The Life and Times

Of

Kitty Wilkinson

By

Michael Kelly

First published 2000 by Countyvise Limited,
14 Appin Road, Birkenhead, Merseyside, CH41 9HH

Copyright © 2000 Michael Kelly

The right of Michael Kelly to be identified as the author of this work has been asserted by
him in accordance with the Copyright, Design and Patents Act 1988.

British Library Cataloguing in Publication Data.
A Catalogue record for this book is available from the British Library.

ISBN 1 871201 08 X

Dedicated
to
My Mother and Father

Acknowledgements

In writing this book I have received most generous help. I am especially indebted to Mr. Thomas Morley for all the help and guidance during the four years it has taken me to prepare this memoir of Kitty Wilkinson.

I should like to express my gratitude to John and Molly Boyd for the hours they spent reading and correcting my manuscript and giving me the benefit of their advice. Also I would like to thank John Boyd for his photographic skills. I owe a special debt to Canon Nicholas Fryling, Rector of Liverpool for his encouragement and help in reading my manuscript and to Margaret Galvin, editor of 'Ireland's Own' for publishing my article 'The Great Kitty Wilkinson'

I would like to thank Mr. Bernard Morgan for his knowledge of Liverpool Irish History and for his unwavering assistance. I would like to thank the staff of the Public Records Office, Central Library Liverpool for the help and assistance during the last four years. Also I would like to thank Emma Challinor archivist of the Rathbone Papers, Sydney Jones Library, The University of Liverpool, for her very valuable assistance.

I am also indebted to John E Moore, archivist, and the staff of The Maritime Archives & Library, Merseyside Maritime Museum who drew my attention to material I should otherwise have missed. I should also like to thank them for permission to reproduce the William Morris Sea Chart of Liverpool Bay.

I should like to thank Roberta Zonghi, Curator of Rare Books Boston Public Library Boston Massachusetts, United States of America for under taking the search for the biographical article on Mr. Joseph Tuckerman. I would also like to thank the Librarian at the Caton branch of the City of Lancaster Library.

Last but not least I would like to thank my friends who have had to put up with me.

In 1927 'The Right Hon. T.P. O'Conner, M.P.'
wrote:

The self-devotion of this woman instinctive,
untaught, uninspired by any body but her own
brave and beautiful character-to the relief of
suffering and want is really an incredible story. She
seems like some 'hound of heaven' to pursue
misery, suffering woman, half starved children,
wherever they might be hidden.

She may be described as the discoverer of the
methods of fighting the terrible scourge of cholera
when it came to Liverpool in 1832.

1

Catherine Seaward
1785-1794

Catherine (Kitty) Seaward was born into a skilled working class family in Derry, Ireland, 1785. Her mother was engaged in spinning and lace making and was competent in reading and writing. The occupation of her father is not known although it has been suggested that he was a soldier. Derry city is the main town of Londonderry it stands on a hill near where the River Foyle falls into Lough Foyle. It is ninety-five miles Northwest of Belfast, the chief industries at that time were flour milling, shipbuilding, bacon curing and the making of linen clothes.

Ireland during the Eighteenth Century had its own Parliament, was politically and geographically, a united country. However it was in the firm grip of England and unrest and poverty was in all quarters. It was around this time that 'The Society of United Irishmen' came into existence. The main aim of the society was to bring all Irishmen together with electoral reform and the extirpation of English influence. At its foundation the society stood broadly on the principles of Thomas Paine's "Rights of Man" (published, 1792). Its aim was to bring all men Protestant and Catholic together. However the Society of United Irishmen and its leaders were put down after 1796 on the orders of Westminster.

George III was on the throne, William Pitt was Prime Minister and England had been drawn into war with France in February 1793. Eighteenth-century Ireland still retained its own language, but the land had long been divided up into, large estates by people who spoke only English.

It was in Derry that Catherine spent the first nine years of her life under the influence of her parents. Catherine had a younger brother and baby sister when her parents were making plans to leave Derry, for Liverpool in 1794. Although she would never see Ireland again her childhood memories and experiences in Derry were the foundation that would carry her through life to face whatever the future had in store.

Liverpool was becoming a vast seaport and in 1751 the total tonnage of the British and foreign vessels that entered the port amounted to 65,406. In 1791, (just before the French war) the tonnage had risen to 539,676 and in 1835 to 1,768,426. The town had a population of about 60,000 in 1794 having doubled since 1760. However from 1794 to 1831 the population of the borough had risen to 165,000.

The immediate result of this immense growth was a steady expansion of the dock system, which until 1825 continued to be owned and directed by the Town Council. Liverpool during the time of Catherine's impending arrival was like a new frontier's town, people starting to pour in from everywhere. With it they brought hope, fear, greed, and honesty, yet for all the problems that people would encounter it was an exciting time. Most people had their faces pushed into the dirt by those who exploited them, some grew rich in this gold rush and the rest tried to survive and build a new future.

Shipbuilding was at its height during the last quarter of the eighteenth century. The yards to the north and south of the docks were famous for the slaving clippers, which they turned out. The yards were also employed between 1778 and 1811 for the building of no less than twenty-one vessels of various types for the Royal Navy.

From that time on the shipbuilding industry slowly went into decline. This period also saw the rise and fall of the whale fishery and oil refineries. It was in 1764 that the Greenland whale fishery began, with three vessels. It reached its height in 1788, when twenty-one ships of 6,485 tons in total, left Liverpool for Greenland. Between 1810 and 1816 there were only two whalers belonging to the port and in 1823 the last survivor made its last voyage.

James Stonehouse "The Streets of Liverpool" wrote:

> *Fish as an article of food was more thought of and in greater request in olden times than at present. From the religious faith of the people, they were constrained to consume fish at particular seasons of the year, and on many particular occasions.*

Salmon was so plentiful in the Mersey that Liverpool was able to sell it to other towns. Up to forty-five other types of fish were reported to be in the river. At one time herrings were caught in great quantities.

The fishery while it existed gave employment to a large oil refining factory beside the Queens Dock and the smell of the whale oil would permeate the air along the waterfront. The herring fishery also gave a great deal of employment and several curing houses existed in the town. At one time curing houses were sited in Wallasey and Garston. James Stonehouse also wrote:

The disturbance of the Mersey waters by the innumerable steamships and vessels constantly present on their surface, and their pollution by the Manchester dye-works, the sewage of the places they pass, and the reckless and improvident conduct of the fishermen themselves. They have all conduced to destroy the finny tribes that once made these waters their habitation.

The fishing industry deserted the port, to be concentrated at the east-coast ports and vanished entirely by 1835. The town had three iron foundries, but they could not stand the competition from the coal field towns. However the river that flowed down to the sea was the life blood of the town and the people its energy. It was also the gateway to the New World, for the goods manufactured in the towns of Lancashire and Yorkshire and further afield.

The rich and the poor lived alongside one another, the rich in the larger houses. The wealthiest merchants lived above their cellar warehouses. The town had narrow and crooked streets, even the main streets were no more than six yards wide, heaps of rubbish and refuse littered the thorough-fare. There were many brothels and taverns, slave ships and their crews were also a regular feature in the port of Liverpool.

In 1795 a cynical observer left us with an invaluable picture of the Liverpool of his day. He calculated that every seventh house in the town was open for the sale of liquor.

The devotion of the lower order of people to their Baccan-alian orgies is such as to give employment to thirty-seven large and extensive breweries.

The town with a population so degraded and so drink-sodden was reinforced by the rough and desperate privateers-men and slavers and was inevitably turbulent and unruly. The streets of Liverpool were constantly the scenes of riots and open fights, especially in the days of the press gang. The same observer wrote:

The pressgang was something calculated to strike fear into a stout man's heart. At their head there was generally a rakish, dissipated, but determined looking officer, in a very seedy uniform and shabby hat. And what follows! Fierce, savage, stern, villainous-looking fellows were they, as ready to cut a throat as eat their breakfast. What an uproar their appearance always made in the streets! The men scowled at them as they passed; the women openly scoffed at them; the children screamed and hid themselves behind doors or fled round corners.

If a man were to be seized by the press gang, he would be treated like a common felon, taken from his home and family. Married men would never see their wives and children again as they were taken away to a prison ship. When the ship was full with its human cargo it would be taken to another port. The men would then be divided among the vessels of war which were in need of men. A Liverpool observer in 1885 wrote that the Press-gang brought terror to wives and children in the town.

The wife widowed, with a husband yet alive; children orphaned by the forcible abduction of their fathers. There were many in those days, not only naval men, but statesmen and legislators, who venerated the pressgangs as one of the pillars and institutions of the country.

The lives of families and children in particular meant very little to those in charge. The people of the town did fight back, the same observer wrote, that the people would take on the press gangs at their own game:

Sometimes, too, the press gangers would get into the wrong box, and, take the wrong sow by the ear, by seizing an American sailor or carpenter, and then there was to be a squall. The bells from the shipbuilding yards would boom out their warning call in the later case, and thousands would muster to set their companion at liberty. A press-

gang man was occasionally tarred and feathered in those days, when caught alone.

The ships that had helped to put down the 1798 rebellion in Ireland were returning to the Mersey. On Sunday morning, October 12, 1798, a gun fired by one of the ships, in saluting the town, happened to be loaded with shot (canon ball) which entered the town near the old dock-gates. Unfortunately several people were standing in its path. The ball first carried off the arm of a cooper, passed through the body of Mr. Treasure, mate of the ship William, then struck the head of a roper, whom it killed on the spot. It afterwards struck the wall of a house at the east-end of the Old Dock and terminated its unfortunate course in Hanover Street.

Another observer commenting on the population of the town wrote:

The great influx of Irish and Welsh, of whom the great number of the inhabitants at present consists, came to inhabit the mean and dirty streets from every part of the British Isles.

It was after the horrors of the 1798 rebellion in Ireland that the immigration of poor Irish people began on a large scale.

The Scots were also well represented but on a smaller scale to the Irish and Welsh. John Gladstone, who came to Liverpool in 1787, from north of the border became an outstanding merchant prince. Towards the end of the century, the rich merchants began to desert the old houses. One of those was Mr. John Gladstone who was the father of William Ewart Gladstone, Prime Minister of Great Britain between 1868-1874. He moved into his new house in 62 Rodney Street just before 1798.

Other merchants moved to the countryside of Everton Hill and Toxteth Park even as far afield as Childwall and Allerton, which was about three miles from the town. The ending of the Eighteenth Century was going well for the merchant class.

William Rathbone was another prominent merchant who displayed concern for the poor of the town with his charity work.

Those who came from privileged backgrounds, were the people who had come to make their fortunes. They were Merchants who knew how to buy and they would sell anything, which would make them a profit. This included Slaves, sugar, cotton, timber, salt, etc and the goods produced by manufacturing industries of Lancashire.

They saw themselves first and foremost as merchants, rather than manufacturers. It was the merchants who had for a long time held a position in the upper English social hierarchy. They did not in the main employ many people in using the means of production and they were not normally large-scale employers of labour.

Great wealth had come; but only to a few, the thirst for money seemed to be the only thing of interest to the town. However a great majority of the inhabitants had little share of this new wealth. A visitor to the town remarked, "all the new towns of the north which had been created by the industrial revolution were hideous enough, but none more dreadful than Liverpool".

Robert Burns, the great Scottish poet who died in 1796, remarked to his brother, "that he could not conceive a more mortifying picture of human life than a man seeking work." A verse from his poem "A Man Was Made To Mourn" reads.

"O Death, the poor man's dearest friend,
The kindest and the best,
Welcome the hour my aged limbs
Are laid with thee at rest!
The great, the wealthy, fear thy blow,
From pomp and pleasure torn;
But oh, a blest relief to those
That weary-laden mourn!"

In the old quarter of the town the houses deserted by the merchants or thriving tradesmen came to be crowded by a swarming multitude of poor people. The cellars once used as warehouses became the homes of whole families. Even the houses inhabited by well-to-do people were commonly let out as dwellings. In 1790 a survey of the town showed that there were 8,148 inhabited houses, of which 1,728 had inhabited cellars. No less than 6,780 persons dwelt in them almost four persons to every cellar.

The freedom of movement was restricted for those at the lower end of the scale, but even for those who could afford it travelling was a nightmare. Only one coach per week travelled between Liverpool and London with passengers sitting up for two nights. A popular way of travel was by the Eastham Boats, according to an advertisement giving details of this service.

The situation of Liverpool affords a speedy and safe conveyance to Chester and all parts of North Wales, by means of these boats, which are large, safe, commodious and strong. They leave the Dry Dock every day about two hours before high water for Eastham.

Further details informed passengers of the benefits of the service.

A stage constantly attends to carry passengers, parcels, &c. to Chester. The safe way to secure the coach is to take your places in the Eastham boat-house on the dock the day before they are wanted, otherwise a passenger may be disappointed of an inside place; for without this precaution they will sometimes find them previously engaged.

The fare by the coach and the boat, was three shillings and sixpence for passage in the best cabin, one shilling in the second. The town had another form of water navigation, the Liverpool and Leeds canal. Coal from the mining towns was brought along its length every hour of the day and night, for the use of its inhabitants. The town was very proud of its facilities for passengers travelling on the canal packets. An advertisement reads.

"On this canal several packets are passing and repassing to Wigan and parts adjacent, the distance of about thirty-two miles, which they perform in about seven hours. The horses employed are not equalled by any in the kingdom on such service."

Comfort and the needs of the passengers were uppermost in the service provided by the Packet Company.

The elegance and construction of those packets are great allurements to the passengers. They not only rival, but are in general superior to those on the Bridgewater navigation; they sail every morning at eight o'clock to Wigan with passengers and parcels, arrive there about four, return from thence at seven o'clock the next morning and reach Liverpool at three o'clock in the afternoon.

Liverpool also had regular sailings to Ireland and had secured more of the Irish trade to the detriment of Parkgate on the River Dee. Parkgate for many years was the only conveyance to Ireland, except from Holyhead in Wales. Stagecoaches carried people to many parts of the Kingdom, that is if you were able to afford the cost of travelling by coach. Most people would have to walk, Horse drawn wagons could be seen everywhere on the roads leading up from the docks carrying their loads to every part of the country.

It was lamented in 1795 that "Liverpool is the only town in England of any pre-eminence that has not one single erection or endowment for the advancement of science, the cultivation of the arts, or the promotion of useful knowledge". A public library was eventually set up and every subscriber was to pay five guineas on admission. An Academy for drawing and painting was attempted in a room over the library. It was also to encourage lectures in anatomy and architecture. However this venture failed, the

President and committee let it be known that, "the attempt proved the mere phantom of the day, the Judicious few, found a very weak support from a body of people, whose inclinations could be influenced to encourage the promotion of sciences".

The architectural character and appearance of the area in 1794 was that of a small town. However St Nicholas's Church was an exception and stood out like a guiding light on the banks of the Mersey looking out to the open sea. There was fomerly in the Churchyard, a statue dedicated to St. Nicholas. It was said that:

Seamen of Romish superstition offered prayers as they went to sea, to implore the Saint's meditation with the virgin, for a successful voyage and safe return.

With the Church being near the river, the bells had a pleasing effect and were generally rung on the safe arrival of fleets, or of any particular vessel. The church was mentioned in the town books, viz. 11 March 1611. Other buildings of importance are the Public Infirmary standing at the top of Shaw's Brow. It was opened to receive patients on the 15th March 1749. The Seamen's Hospital was later added to the infirmary and opened in 1752 as a charity. It was decided that its main function was "For the maintenance of decayed seamen of the port of Liverpool, their wives and children". The seamen paid towards the running cost. It was principally supported by the monthly allowance of sixpence, which every seaman sailing from the port is by Act of Parliament to pay out of his wages.

The Blue Coat Hospital made its first appearance in 1709, under the name of a charity school, providing for forty boys and ten girls. However there was one institution to strike fear into the hearts of every member of the community, it was the workhouse. It had first appeared in College Lane, off Hanover Street, but the ever-increasing destitute people in the town brought the need for larger premises.

Brownlow Hill was the chosen spot for the new institution and the fears that the poor had in the past would increase tenfold. Towards the end of the century it was decided that the blind be cared for in a different manner. In 1790 the Asylum for the Indigent Blind was opened and an observer wrote, "If there is a state of human wretchedness deserving commiseration, it is that of blindness, united in poverty: without the ability, or the means of obtaining instruction in such mechanical labour."

People standing in the centre of Liverpool, would need only a brisk walk to find themselves in the countryside in any direction. Windmills could be seen on the outskirts of the town covering much of the landscape and they were used for grinding corn. Unlike the towns of Lancashire, Liverpool had only about 5% of the population employed in manufacturing. Small-scale handicraft's production employed many people. The Town's manufacturers were mainly involved in items necessary for the construction and equipment of ships. Around this time more than 3000 shipwrights were employed almost full time repairing and building ships.

Liverpool had tobacco and snuff manufacturing, red and white herring houses, three iron foundries and pipe makers. There was also coach building, cabinet making, and watch making in the town. The south west of the town had a salt works, which for many years had produced salt of an excellent quality. The salt works were found to be a great nuisance to the inhabitants and removed to Garston about four miles from the town. Although the people of the town had to work hard for low wages, there were those who had organised themselves to relieve them of their hard earned cash. An excerpt from a contemporary Journal read:

"An extensive porter brewery, in Scotland Road has been lately established; which promises to furnish as good a quality of liquor as the London breweries."

With the ever-increasing importance of the town to the nation and its increasing population, also came the need to build a new prison.

The newest and most splendid building in the town was the new jail which was just north of the Pierhead, at the beginning of Great Howard Street. It was described as:

The "Temple of the Goddess Lavern" where, it rises in all the glare of ostentatious majesty.

It had more than twice the cells of Newgate prison, and was capable of holding more than half the inhabitants of Liverpool at that time. The jail also held many French prisoners of war. There were no adequate police during this period and in the daytime none at all. At night there were a few old and feeble watchmen who paraded the streets. It was not until 1836 that Liverpool had a full time Police Force.

The Watch Committee as a result of the 1835 Reform Act approached Michael James Whitty and offered him the post of head constable. Thus not only was the Liverpool's first Chief Constable, the founder of the police force but also Fire Brigade in Liverpool. Michael was training for the Priesthood before he left County Wexford in Ireland, for London. After a spell in Journalism he settled in Liverpool. Then after retiring from the police force he founded the Liverpool Daily Post, which is still in existence today.

The town did have its leisure facilities. There was the old "Theatre" in Williamson Square, opened in 1772. It was built by the subscription of thirty gentlemen, who received 5% of the respective investment. They were also entitled to attend every night performance in every part of the house. It was described at the time, "as complete a Theatre as any of the metropolis, and generally supplied with a good set of comedians." The Music Hall was another place of entertainment which was situated in Bold

Street. There were twelve concerts a year and a festival of music once every three years. The subscription to the concerts was two guineas a year.

The Public Markets of Liverpool were supplied from Ireland, Wales and from the Isle of Man. Cattle were imported alive, together with swine bacon and butter. The Isle of Man, Anglesey and many parts of North-Wales and Cheshire sent a great number of live poultry of all sorts. Information supplied by the meat marketing trade assured the town that:

The demand for beef, live sheep and pigs, for supply of the shipping is here very great. There is a pretty breed of sheep in many parts of Lancashire, with black faces and feet that afford most excellent mutton.

It also went on to explain the good practices of the local trade compared to that of other towns.

The market is also plentifully supplied from Derbyshire and North Wales, with sheep that yield to none in goodness in flavour. Veal is fine and well tasted, but not in general so white as in many other parts of the kingdom. The butchers however, to the honour of Liverpool, do not use the filthy custom of blowing the meat when hot, to inflate the fat and juices with stinking breath of the operator, a practice too general in London and many other parts.

The never ending stream of people were still pouring into Liverpool trying to find work and that flow would go on well into the next century. Most of the new arrivals came from rural backgrounds. They came unprepared for the ways of town life and the terror that was to greet them. People were scratching in the dirt like hens in a chicken run for a few crumbs that would help to sustain life. Gone was the close-knit community of rural life. Their innocence had led them into a rat race of no return because of their poverty.

The town brought together the Irish, Welsh, Scots, and the Lancashire people. The strong Celtic cultures blended well with their Lancashire neighbours and brought about a temperament and dialect unlike any other. Liverpool was no better or worse than any other town during the early part of the industrial revolution. Every man and woman came looking for a better future for themselves and their children. Some wanted to be rich, others just the chance to be able to feed themselves and their families.

Entering the narrow channel into Liverpool bay from the Irish Sea in the 1790s on a sailing ship, could be a risky business. Sandbanks lay in wait for any ship that was blown off course in a gale or during bad visibility during the day, or in the darkness of night. Even the biggest sailing ship in those days would not be much more than 300 tons and the navigation aids on board ship were of a basic nature. A fierce gale could toss a ship about like a piece of driftwood onto the waiting sandbanks. Navigation was through a much narrower channel in those days.

Looking out to the right from a ship before entering the River Mersey one sees the Wirral peninsula and beyond the River Dee which divides the peninsula from Wales. On a clear day you can see the green Welsh Mountains. Over to the left is Formby Point on the Lancashire coastline and Liverpool ten miles further on. Formby had then the only life boat station in the area. The lifeboat was nothing more than an open boat. From the position of the lifeboat station it was possible to see across the sandbanks at the mouth of the Dee even in bad weather by the use of a telescope. Green vegetation covered the whole coastline on both sides of the Mersey.

Catherine Seaward (Kitty Wilkinson) (b. Derry 1785; d. Liverpool November 1860.)

Ordnance Survey Map of Liverpool Bay

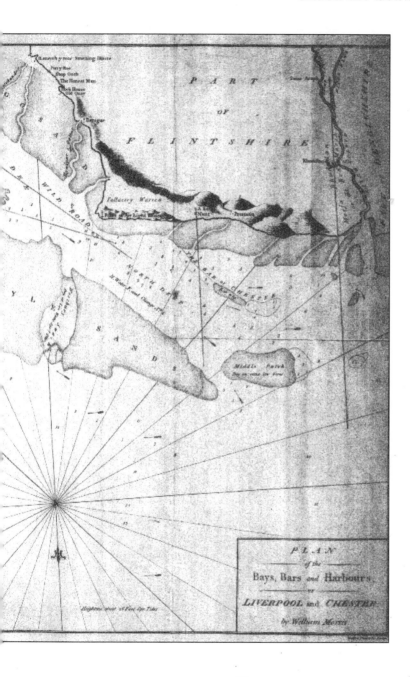

Kitty Wilkinson

2

Liverpool
1785-1794

One can only speculate that on the day of their departure from Derry the Seaward family must have had mixed feelings, leaving their home and a country in turmoil. News would no doubt have reached them that Liverpool was a rapidly expanding town which would give them an opportunity to create a better future for their young family. A man would need a stout heart to take a young family on a sea voyage of over two hundred miles in 1794, but Liverpool it had to be.

The Seawards set sail on a winter morning in early February when the sun was rising. Catherine and her younger brother were exploring the workings of this small sailing ship while her mother sat cradling her infant child. Mr. Seaward paid more attention to Catherine and her brother making sure they kept out of the way of the ships crew. A more pleasant day the family could not have wished for, it was like a spring day and everybody was thankful for a few hours of sunshine. An arctic tern was perched on top of the main mast and appeared to be looking down at the passengers below then, she spread her wings and headed back towards the main land. The ship was making good time under full sail with a crew good at harnessing the wind.

As the evening closed in, the Seawards and the rest of the deck passengers fell silent. The flapping of the sails against a soft breeze could be heard in tune with the rest of the ship's rigging. Vibrations and creaking deck planking sent forth a steady rhythm. The slapping of the sea against the ship's bow and the steady surge of the ship made up this orchestral performance of tranquillity.

As the night moved on the Seaward children grew restless, however the restlessness was no problem to their parents. They had packed a good store of food and water, enough to last the journey's end. The food had a calming effect on Catherine and the younger children. By midnight most of the passengers lying about the deck had settled down to await the early morn. The ships bos'un could be heard giving orders to the members of the crew still on watch, His voice had lost some of the power that it had during the daylight hours. The noise of the ship's rigging seemed to grow louder not having to compete with the sounds of excited passengers.

It was a long night sitting or lying down on the open deck for the Seaward family and the rest of the deck passengers. The sails took on a different colour as the dawn broke stirring some of the deck passengers from their slumber. Once again the sun was rising giving of its warm rays. Ahead lay England which had just come into sight of the observant onlookers. Then without warning the bright blue sky gave way to darkening clouds and this small sailing ship was being tossed about. The rain followed, and light drops were soon swallowed up by the dry sails and deck planking. The wind followed growing with intensity and parents gathered their children into their arms and a frightening silence befell the once happy passengers.

The ship's crew was doing its best to keep a steady course as she came into Liverpool Bay from the Irish sea but they felt it was a battle already lost. The rain was lashing against the sails as the crew tried to bring them under their control and the sky grew darker. The ship's Master was fearful that they would be carried onto the sand banks that lay on each side of the narrow channel which leads to the River Mersey. By this time screams could be heard from the frightened passengers in the cabins and those on deck tried to hold onto their children in the howling wind and rain.

The gale increasing its pressure on the small ship snapped the main mast sending it across the deck. The ship started to list to starboard taking it towards the Wirral Peninsula and away from the entrance to the Mersey. People on the shore across the bay at Formby could see the floundering ship. The crew of the only life boat in the area, stationed at Formby Point, put to sea in the raging gale. It was no more than a large rowing boat fighting heavy seas to get to the stricken ship. By the time they reached her the ship had been driven further to the west and came to rest on the treacherous Hole Bank at the entrance of the River Dee.

Catherine and the rest of her family were holding on for dear life with the rest of the passengers and ship's crew. The heavy seas soon broke the back of this small sailing ship and she was starting to sink when the life boat reached her. Catherine and her mother and the two younger children were taken onto the life boat but there was no trace of her father. However the danger was not yet over for the rest of the Seaward family, Mrs Seaward was holding her infant child in her arms as the life boat was fighting its way back to the nearest shore. Then without any warning the gale force wind snatched the baby from the arms of Mrs Seaward and it was washed overboard. It is uncertain as to what happened to Kitty's father during that terrible storm. It is possible that in trying to save the lives of his wife and children, he perished on the stricken ship.

It was recorded during this period that, during a violent storm in the 1790s a vessel was seen in distress and men could be observed lashed to the mast. Five boat men put to sea and by the time they reached the doomed vessel, part of it had sunk. The crew of the sinking vessel fell into the rescue boat and were brought safely ashore. This may well have been the sailing ship that Catherine and her family sailed on as passengers

Picton, Memorials of Liverpool Vol. I, contains an interesting paragraph relating to a very severe storm:

> *On February 4, 1794, the town was visited by a dreadful hurricane which committed very severe damage, and filled the river with wrecks.*

It is not hard to imagine the suffering of Mrs. Seaward finding herself in a strange town with two children and no home. The Seawards did not seem the sort of family who would leave their home in Derry with three young children in the off chance of finding work and a place to stay. They were a skilled and literate family, therefore doubtful, that they could have been persuaded to leave their homeland on a chance that they might better themselves. There is the possibility that Mr. Seaward had a position mapped out before he left home with his family. Catherine was later to become known as Kitty. Winefride R. Rathbone in her memoir of Kitty published as a children's book wrote:

> *Catherine's father was a soldier and that was the reason for them travelling to Liverpool.*

If this was the case, any plans that the family had for a new life in the town, would have disappeared with the death of Mr. Seaward.

In 1927 Herbert Rathbone published an edited manuscript of the life of Kitty, the manuscript was found amongst the possessions of Mrs. Rathbone, wife of William Rathbone. It was believed that Kitty was the author of this work, whether by her own hand, or by the many notes that Mrs. Rathbone made during her visits to Kitty. Reference is made to Kitty's mother landing in Liverpool with her children:

When Mrs Seaward was crossing with her children from Ireland, the vessel in which they were passengers was wrecked; the crew and passengers escaped into a small boat, and with difficulty reached the shore; but, while they were struggling with the storm, the youngest child, an infant, was washed out of her poor mother's arms by a wave that struck them.

Although Mrs. Seaward recovered from the shock of this dreadful ordeal, resulting in the suffering and exposure she had undergone the nightmare of this tragedy was later to bring on a fever. The result of this was, her health was never the same again. The physician who attended her said that in all probability in the course of a few years, she would become both blind and insane.

After their ordeal was over the Seawards settled in Denison Street in the north-end of the town. Denison Street was still occupied by professional and trades people during the 1790s and they rented out their cellars to the poor of the town. The whole of the area north of Liverpool was unspoilt during Kitty's early years in the town. As far as the eye could see there were fields and meadows; the people who lived along the banks of the Mersey worked the land. After settling in, Mrs. Seaward soon found work for herself and Kitty. They were employed by a Mrs. Lightbody to do domestic work. However it was not long before Mrs. Lightbody realised that the Seawards had more to offer. Mrs. Seaward was offered the job of teaching the servants and other employees how to spin and the art of lace making. Herbert R. Rathbone, tells us that:

Distress and poverty, the consequence of her mother's ill-health, was thus the lot of little Kitty in her early childhood, but they were the means by which, as she herself says: (I was blessed, as few poor children are blessed, for they introduced me to a blind friend who became like a mother to me.)

This friend was Mrs. Lightbody, an aged and infirm lady who found her happiness in relieving the sufferings and supplying the wants of the poor. Although Kitty continued to live with her mother, she spent the day in Mrs. Lightbody's house assisting the servants in such household tasks as she was able to perform.

Because of her blindness Mrs. Lightbody came to rely more on Kitty of whom she became very fond. One of Kitty's duties was to help the old lady in her charity work but due to the poor state of her health Mrs. Lightbody was carried about in a sedan chair. Kitty would help by knocking on doors of the poor so that Mrs. Lightbody could speak to them. Mrs. Lightbody's family were the owners of land in the Vauxhall and Kirkdale area situated about two miles north of central Liverpool. Kitty and her mother would only have a short walk to work each morning. When Kitty and her family settled into Denison Street, it was the last street in the north of the town. Later the green fields would give way to what was to become the Vauxhall District.

It would seem from Herbert Rathbone's edited manuscript, that Kitty's childhood was one of poverty and distress:

Her mother though skilled in spinning and lace making was, because of her poor state of health, unable to earn enough money for the adequate support of her children.

Kitty's mother must have had moderate health for some time after the tragedy which befell her family, to be able to pass on her skills of spinning and lace making. A number of accounts over the years have credited Mrs. Lightbody with teaching Kitty to read and write. However this could hardly have been the case knowing that Mrs. Lightbody was a blind lady. In the eighteenth century there was very little provision for the lower class to receive any form of education.

The early years for Kitty in Liverpool may have been a happy period in her young life, spent on the outskirts of the town, but we will never be sure how she felt at that time. However Kitty had the benefit of living in the countryside on the banks of the Mersey giving her a clear view of the Wirral peninsula and Welsh mountains beyond. Ships lying at anchor were a regular sight, their sails stowed away leaving the masts and rigging bare like trees that had shed their leaves in autumn.

Many years would pass by before the docks and warehouses were built restricting the view across the Mersey.

The new life that the Seaward's had made for themselves was not to last, misfortune was to strike once more. Kitty's mother was taken ill, the tragedy of their experience on that fateful day sailing from Ireland had taken its toll. Herbert Rathbone records the events at that time.

When Kitty was about eleven years old her Mother's health became so much worse that she was obliged to go into the Infirmary at Liverpool, and after leaving that institution she went over to Ireland to be with her own friends. Her two children, Kitty and a little boy, were left behind at this time. Kitty was a delicate child, and Mrs Lightbody thought it would be very desirable for her to leave town and go and live in the country. With this view she sent the two children to a cotton mill at Caton, Lancaster (which belonged to Mrs, Hudson, a relative of hers, and which was.a pleasant and healthy situation), to remain during their mother's absence.

If Mrs. Lightbody was in a position to have Kitty and her brother looked after in the country, why did they not stay where they were? They were already living and working in a pleasant situation on the banks of the Mersey. There is no evidence of Kitty's mother returning to Ireland. With the deterioration in her health it is doubtful if she would have been able to sustain a sea voyage of over two hundred miles. Had she returned to Derry she would have had to travel in a similar type of sailing ship that had already brought so much tragedy into her life.

In the event of a breakdown in the health of Mrs. Seaward, she would be of little use to an employer. She was a woman dependent on her wages, from her labour, to keep a roof over her head. So the only other option would be the Liverpool workhouse rather than return to her native country. It is also most unlikely that Mrs Lightbody would have made arrangements for Kitty and her brother to be sent to Caton. It is more likely that it would have been the overseer at the workhouse, who would make arrangements for Kitty to be indentured and sent to Low Mill, Caton.

Kitty by this time was eleven years old and those in charge at the workhouse had the right to transport children from an early age to a cotton mill. This could be done without the parents' consent because they were a burden on the Parish. As for Kitty remaining at Low Mill only until her mother's health improved, this was not the case. Kitty would have to sign indentures binding her to this new employer for ten years until the age of twenty-one.

Herbert Rathbone also informs us that before Kitty went to her new residence:

> *Mrs Lightbody gave her as a parting remembrance, a copy of Wyatt's Hymns for Children, desiring her to learn those which pleased most, and to send word of those to her she chose. In this manner she hoped, though far away, to influence her little charge for good.*

This gift to Kitty on the departure seems to suggest that she was a religious person. Or was Mrs. Lightbody hoping to influence her young friend by asking her to read and learn the hymns?

Kitty Wilkinson

3

Low Mill, Caton
1796-1806

Two years after arriving in Liverpool, Kitty left the town together with other homeless children to work in the cotton mills of Lancashire. The children were not consulted about the move, so the decision was taken without their consent. They were taken on a sixty mile journey by horse-drawn wagon to the ancient market town of Lancaster. The Industrial Revolution made Lancashire the world's leading producer of cotton textiles, and Lancashire was to become one of the centres of the newly emerging cotton industry being situated along the north western coast of England along the Irish Sea. The coast of Lancashire and its environment was ideal for the cotton industry supplied through the 'Port of Liverpool'.

The cotton mills were one corner of the slave trade and the children had become very much part of the slave market. After a short rest in the town, Kitty and the rest of the homeless children had another four miles to travel before they reached the village of Caton and Low Mill. The Mill commanded a view of the Lune Valley, which is still a place of rare beauty bordering on the Forest of Bowland.

A treasured feature of the village, is the ancient oak tree with the stepped stones shaded beneath it. This tree is reputed to be a thousand years old, and tradition has it that monks displayed their Lune fish catches for sale on the stones beneath it.

During the 1790s most of the "apprentices" employed at Low Mill were recruited from workhouses in the Lancashire and Yorkshire areas and some even as far away as London. This practice was widely used by mill owners in Lancashire, Yorkshire and Cheshire. Children like Kitty had to sign an "Indenture" which bound them to live at the Apprentice House and to spend the next ten years working in the cotton mill.

Children much younger than Kitty were also subjected to this enforced labour which would continue until they reached the age of twenty-one. After putting their signature or mark to the "Indenture" no child was allowed to leave their place of employment. The mill owner had total control over the children; they could only leave with the consent of their employer or with the permission of a magistrate. It was a rare thing for any boy or girl to be given their freedom before they reached twenty-one.

The apprentices would not be paid any wage in spite of the long working hours. The mill owners considered it necessary only to feed, clothe and provide accommodation. This, they considered, was their sole responsibility towards the general welfare of the children. Kitty was described as a 'delicate child,' which was the main reason for sending her to Low Mill at Caton, here she was to enjoy the benefits of the countryside!!

Had Kitty been a delicate child, she would never have been able to work the fourteen hour day, six days a week, at Low Mill. The children saw very little of the countryside as they were marshalled to and from the mill. On leaving their place of work, they would be led back to the 'Apprentice House' and locked in for the night.

Low Mill, Caton

Low Mill was built by Thomas Hodgson, a Caton man, in 1784.

He bought a farm on the side of the Lune Valley for this purpose. Building it close to the river gave him the required water for the 'large water wheel' on the side of the mill that would give him the power to work his machinery. The farmhouse was converted into an apprentice house thus enabling Hodgson to import labour. Caton was a very remote area and labour was difficult to find, so orphans and other unwanted children, many from Liverpool, were brought in.

There is no reason to suppose that Low Mill was any better or worse than any of the other mills operating at that time. Kitty started her "Apprenticeship", long before the first Factory Act was brought into force for the preservation of the health and morals of apprentices, etc. employed in cotton mills and other factories. Legislation was not in place until the Factories Act 1802 which would give employees some protection. Sadly however most employers disregarded the Factories Act.

Conditions such as payment of wages, hours of work, or the age of workers, was left to the employers to determine. It is not therefore surprising, that a great number of workers were treated with contempt and were forced to endure an unbelievably harsh regime. Under the new Act child employees were not allowed to work more than 12 hours a day and no later than 9 p.m. They also had to be taught the 'three Rs' during their working hours. Very few factory owners observed the new ruling and those who did made sure it was limited. Nevertheless in later years Kitty was frequently quoted about the fondness she felt for Low Mill, one such remark was:

If ever there was a heaven upon earth it was that apprentice house, where we were brought up in such ignorance of evil.

The conditions in most, if not all, of the apprentice houses in the Cotton Mills were certainly not "A Heaven Upon Earth." It would be difficult to expect, that Low Mill, was an exception to the rule. Many of the documents surviving from Quarry Bank Mill at Styal, Cheshire tell a harrowing story.

The Apprentice House where the children lived divided the girls from the boys placing girls in rooms on one side and boys on the other. The boys would sleep in two or three small rooms in order to allow the house manager and his wife to keep better control. Even so the boys would, quite naturally, get into fights amongst themselves, mainly through boredom.

It is recorded that twenty to thirty girls would sleep in one room after finishing a twelve hour shift. The girls would also be expected to work a further two hours sewing garments before the oil lamps were turned off. The room would have a bucket for use as a toilet; the girls would not be allowed out of the room until morning. The beds resembled large bakers trays, each about four-feet square with high sides. Two girls slept in each bed, the mattress was stuffed with straw and was only changed twice a year: It would not be difficult to imagine what the straw was like after a few months. Some of the children would wet the bed, even then the straw would not be changed. Conditions for the boys would of course be the same, except they would be in smaller groups.

The children worked six days a week and Sunday would be the day when they would be assured of some small respite. However it was not unknown for children to work seven days a week if they were in the employment of a more unscrupulous mill owner. During the hours of darkness the only lighting in the mill was the hundreds of oil lamps. Gas lighting was not in use until long after Kitty left her employment in the cotton mills. In 1806, William Murdock installed 1,000 gas lights in a Manchester cotton mill, but it would be many more years before the rest of the mills had gas lighting.

All the children had to attend church and would have to walk there no matter how far it was from their house. The people living in the village and connected to the mill would also be expected to attend church service. Unless Kitty's master was an exceptional employer she would have received very little education, if any, during her stay there. A school house adjoined the apprentice house, where the boys were taught to read and write in the most basic way. The girls were denied even this most basic learning, but were taught to sew and knit.

We may never be sure what conditions were like at Low Mill as most records of this establishment appear to have been lost or destroyed. However, it is more than likely that Kitty had a good relationship with her employer because she already had the ability to read and write. These and other skills had been passed on by her mother. The encouragement Kitty received from Mrs Lightbody in her reading and writing also helped her through the many years spent at Low Mill. Kitty never again saw the lady who had made such an impression on her, Mrs. Lightbody died when Kitty was twelve. Herbert Rathbone wrote:

> *Mr. Hudson, the manager of the mill, was like a father to the children under his care; not only watching over their mental and moral progress, but frequently devoting his evenings to their amusement, by teaching them and playing with them a variety of games.*

It is possible this man did show some kindness towards the children. However Sunday would be the only time that the children would be allowed out of the apprentice house and that would be under supervision. Kitty remained at the apprentice house until she was eighteen, then like all the other young people she was allowed to take lodging in the nearby village. Living in the village would not be the gateway to total freedom. Kitty would not be allowed to stay away from the village for any reason before or during working hours or without the permission of the master. Kitty enjoyed the freedom to wander in the village and to visit the homes of people with whom she worked.

After the death of Thomas Gregg the mill owner; his son Samuel Gregg took charge of 'Low Mill'. He was married to Hannah Lightbody, who was born in 1767, the daughter of Mrs Lightbody. Many years before Kitty was sent to work in the cotton mills, a young boy by the name of Thomas Rowley, was sent to Quarry Bank mill, situated in the village of Styal in Cheshire. In the Mill's early years about half the jobs were done by children. In 1785 Thomas Rowley was the first pauper apprentice sent to Quarry Bank Mill by the Overseers of the Poor for Newcastle Under Lyme. They sent more than two hundred Indentured young workers to the Mill. However the Indenture was designed to meet the needs of the employer:

> *This Indenture made the twenty-fifth Day of May 1785 Witnesseth, that Thomas Payne, Church Warden of the Parish & Borough of Newcastle in the County of Stafford and Thomas Barrett Overseer of the Poor of the said Parish & Borough by and with the Consent of His Majesty's Justice of the peace for the said Borough, whose Names are hereunto subscribed, have put and placed, and by these Present do put and place Thomas Rowley a poor child of the said Parish Apprentice to Sam Greg Esq. of Manchester in the County Lancaster, Cotton Manufacturer, with him to dwell and serve from the day of the date by these presents, until the said Apprentice shall accomplish his full age of Twenty-one years according to the statute in that case made and provided: During all which Term, the said Apprentice his said Master faithfully shall serve in all lawful Businesses.*

In Witness Where of, the Parties aforesaid to these present indentures interchangeably have set their Hands and Seals the Day and Year first above written.

Thomas Rowley 11 years old

Thomas Rowley's Master was required to provide for his apprentice, competent and sufficient meat, drink, apparel, lodging, washing and other things necessary and fit for an apprentice.

Many accounts have been written about Kitty's time at Low Mill, Caton, giving the impression that it was a wonderful experience for her.

Kitty was seventeen years of age when the Factory Act of 1802 came into force. She was at the age when she would be getting ready to find her own lodgings in Caton village. In all the years Kitty spent at Caton Mill nothing changed in the employment of children and it was not until 1833 that new legislation came about. The Act of 1833 forbid the employment of children under nine years of age in factories and provided 'inter alia' (amongst other things) for an eight hour day for children under the age of thirteen.

After leaving the apprentice house when she was eighteen, Kitty stayed on at Low Mill in Caton village, going to lodge with a woman in the neighbourhood. Kitty was very happy living in the village. Much of this was brought about by the kindness shown by her landlady. She continued to work at the mill until she was turned twenty. Wages fluctuated between ten, and fifteen shillings a week.

During this time news reached Kitty that her mother had returned to Liverpool from Ireland. However it is more likely that she had been released from the Liverpool Workhouse. The health of her mother had not improved over the long years of separation from her children. Kitty, having experienced the suffering of the people and children in the cotton mill, was not willing to leave her mother on her own and she left the security of village life and returned to Liverpool to comfort and look after her afflicted mother.

It must be also remembered that Kitty had a younger brother who was sent with her to Low Mill. However there is no record of him surviving the regime of the mill system. It must have been difficult for Kitty to return to Liverpool now that her years of bondage were over. After all the Lune Valley and its green pastures must have reminded her of the homeland of her childhood.

During the years Kitty was at Low Mill she had heard many stories about Liverpool from the carters who delivered their heavy loads to the mill. The town was thriving and work was plentiful for those who had the skills that were needed and those at the top of the heap were getting richer. However for many it was a sea of poverty and bad housing: Far worse were the tales told by the carters about the cruelty to children in mills throughout Lancashire and beyond. Conditions in the treatment and welfare of young workers had not changed in all the long years Kitty was in the mills.

Long after Kitty left, children would continue to be transported to a life of servitude in the cotton mills. Gradually over the coming years in the courts of inquiry their stories were told. Mr. Robert Blincoe, formally employed in the mills gave evidence to a Bolton Journalist in the 1820s.

'Do you work at a cotton mill?'

Not now. I was bound apprentice to a cotton mill for fourteen years from St. Pancras Parish; then I got my indentures. I worked for five or six years at different mills, but now I have got work of my own. I rent power from a small mill in Stockport and have a room to myself; my business is sheet wadding manufacture.

'Why did you leave off working at the cotton mills?'

I got tired of it, the system is so bad and I had saved a few pounds. I got deformed there; my knees began to bend in when I was fifteen; you see how they are (showing them.) There are many far worse than me at Manchester."
'Can you take exercise with ease?'
"A very little makes me sweat in walking, I have not the strength of those who are straight.

'Have you any children?'

Three.

'Do you send them to factories?'

No, I would rather have them transported. In the first place, they are standing upon one leg, lifting up one knee, a great part of the day, keeping the ends up from the spindle. I consider that this employment makes many cripples; then there is the heat and the dust, then there is so many forms of cruelty used upon them. Then they are so liable to have their fingers catched and to suffer other accidents from the machinery; then the hours is so long, that I have seen them tumble down asleep among the straps and machinery, and so cruelly get hurt. Then I would not have a child of mine there because there is no good morals; there is such a lot of them together that they learn mischief."

'What are the forms of cruelty that you spoke of just now as being practised upon children in factories?'

I have seen the time when two hand-vices of a pound weight each, more or less, have been screwed to my ears, at Lytton mill in Derbyshire. Here are the scars still remaining behind my ears. Then three or four of us have been hung at once on a cross beam above the machinery, hanging by our hands, with out shirts or stockings. Mind, we were apprentices, without father or mother to take care of us, I don't say that they often do that now.

During the early 1800s a number of articles were published on the plight of the 'Apprentices.' Many of those articles and evidence given at courts of inquiry were published by the editor of the 'Aston Chronicle' in 1849. This is an extract of one of those articles about a Parish Prentice at Litton and Cressbrook Mill, Derbyshire, he wrote:

The world has been a rough one to him; but he has battled with it well, and all he has gone through has never lost his manliness. He believes in God, and has not fainted under the heavy burden. Though he has borne much unkindness from his fellow-man, and as an Englishman has found no shield in the law against the wrong done to him by those, who both make law and religion an engine of oppression to the poor, we never heard him speak hatefully of any. The iron has entered deep into his soul; but his feelings are still fresh. He has a child-like mind. His heart is whole. He would do harm to no one, not even to the worst of those who have treated him so ill.

I was born in Hare Street, Bethnal-Green, London, in the year 1805, as I have been told by my grandmother, and was christened in Bethnal-Green Church, in the same year. My father died when I was two years old, leaving two children, my self and Sarah my sister. She was two years older than I. My father was buried in the above Churchyard.

My mother kept us both till I was about five years old, and

*then she took badly in decline, and was taken to the London
Hospital, London Road. My sister and I were taken to the
Bethnal-Green workhouse. She came out of hospital said to
be cured! but a week after leaving the hospital she died.*

Together with about forty other children, the boy was taken to
Whitehaven, in Cumberland. He was no more than six or seven
years of age. They were driven to Paddington canal, where there
was a boat provided to take them. While the children were waiting
to board, he made his escape, and he went straight back to the
workhouse thinking he would be safe. He went to the lodge door
and knocked. When he got in he was knocked down and kicked:
he was then put into the oakum cellar to work with men and
women. He continued to work in the oakum cellar until he was
about ten.

Once again the time came for him to be moved on, when told
that he was a fine lad, The managers of the workhouse asked him
if he would like to go to the country. They told him, he would
soon become a man and earn twenty shillings a week. This was
about three weeks before Christmas 1815. He agreed to go
because he was feeling very uncomfortable in the workhouse. The
move was on a Friday, about one o'clock at noon, in the depth of
winter. They travelled all night and arrived in Buxton at four
o'clock on the Saturday afternoon. A covered cart was waiting for
them there. They all got in and were driven off to the "prentice
house" at Litton Mill, about six miles from Buxton.

They went to work at five the following morning until nine at
night and on a Saturday, untill eleven, then they were sent to
clean the machinery on the Sunday. No time was allowed for
breakfast they would have to eat while working. Further cruelty
was inflicted on the young apprentices by almost daily beatings;
the object of the beatings was to break the spirit. Needham, the
master, had five sons: those young men, together with a man by

the name of Swann an overlooker carried out most of the beatings.

Another such mill was Cressbrook Mill which stands on the east side of the river Wye. Like most of the mills it overlooked some of the finest beauty in the region. It lay in a dale called Monsal Dale. There a spring rises from under a hill which becomes a large Brooke, the area was noted for growing watercress, from whence the mill was named. It was surrounded by a nine feet high wall, it also had an "apprentice" house and the masters house. It was about a mile-and-a-half from Litton Mill, and three miles from Tydeswell. A former apprentice gave information to an inquiry investigating the running of the mills.

We were all fastened in. When we came from the factory at night, we all took our seats, and the master, Newton came in and called every name. We answered to our names. they then brought suppers. The girl's apartment was situated on the north front of the building, a story above us, we had no communication with them at all. Our bedchamber was an old building attached to the "prentice-house". Our beds consisted of a large wooden case, something like a cart frame or a packing case, with boarded bottom, and boarded sides and ends. A parting board came down the middle, east and west; we lay three together, on each side of the bed north and south, six in the double.

Most of the mills had a similar way of working, and their methods of controlling the apprentices were identical. There was great competition in the cotton industry during this period and if mill owners wanted to survive they had to keep costs to a minimum. The machines had to be looked after, but the apprentices could be pushed beyond the limit if necessary. The same apprentice gave an example of this to the enquiry.

We went to our work at six in the morning without anything at all to eat or fire to warm us. For a year after I went we never stopped for breakfast. The breakfast was brought to the mill in tin cans on large trays. It was milk, porridge and oat cake. They brought them into the room, and everyone took a tin and ate his breakfast as he could catch it, working away all the while. We stopped at twelve o'clock, and had an hour for dinner, but had the cleaning to do during that time. It took some of us half an hour to clean and oil the machinery.

Cressbrooke had more than four hundred apprentices, many came from as far afield as the London Parishes of St. Giles, Clerkenwell, and Marylebone. The editor of the Aston Chronicle tells us of another former 'Apprentice' who was enslaved at Cressbrook Mill.

The story was told to him by a poor woman, who spent some years at Cressbrooke Mill. She had read the story of the London 'apprentice' and felt the need to let others know about the treatment which fatherless and friendless girls had to undergo in that house of bitter and cruel bondage, He interviewed many people who had passed through this form of slavery from childhood and wrote:

Who in childhood were thus made to pass through the fire, as an offering to the bloody Moloch, whom we and our fathers have worshipped.

Of those he interviewed all agreed only one-half of the truth had been told. He felt great pity for the woman and the London Apprentice and all the other apprentices that had passed through Cressbrooke mill from the day it opened and he wrote:

That was indeed the hour of power and darkness. How many children were clean murdered will never be known until the day, when, what has been hidden on earth will be brought to light before that righteous God.

The following is an extract from the woman's statement to the editor of the Aston Chronicle.

> *My brother was at Cressbrook Mill two years before me.*
> *He was sent from a Bristol workhouse in the same way as*
> *many other children were - cart-loads at a time. I was then*
> *about eight years old, a very little girl. My mother did not*
> *know where he was for two years. He was taken off in the*
> *dead of night without her knowledge, and the parish officers*
> *would never tell her where he had gone. I think it was the*
> *mother of Joseph Russell who first found out where the*
> *children were, and told my mother. We set off together, my*
> *mother and I, for my father had died in the Brazils, and we*
> *were left dependent on the parish.*

When this young girl and her mother arrived at Cressbrook Mill she and her mother were given the false impression that the boy was being looked after, thus trapping this eight year old to stay at the mill to work alongside her brother. The girl was given a shilling and told to make her mark on a document. Little did she know this would bind her to be enslaved until she reached twenty-one.

The shilling was soon spent, but the beatings and other forms of cruelty soon followed. She quickly learned that she, and the rest of the children would not be allowed to speak during the long working hours. Together with the other apprentices she worked from five in the morning until nine at night. A man by the name of Thomas Birks was in charge of the works. He was encouraged by the master to inflict cruelty on the children and the rest of the workforce. This man was given the name of "Tom-The-Devil," by the apprentices.

4

Return to Liverpool
1807-1815

On arriving in Liverpool, Kitty's first task was to find suitable accommodation for her mother and herself. This proved to be no easy matter, every available space was being taken up by those seeking to build a new life for themselves. Kitty tried to find a place to live in Denison Street so that once again, her mother could be near old friends and neighbours, but no accommodation could be found in the street. Kitty and her mother settled in Frederick Street in the south end of the town. Once the roof over her head was secure her next task was to find work. Although Kitty was a bright young woman, she was not in a position to be choosy in the type of work she would take. The town had changed out of all proportion to the one she had left, when she was eleven. Liverpool was not an orderly town, unlike the village she had left, but it was an exciting place.

People and buildings competed for space and the ever increasing ships on the river waited patiently to unload their cargoes. The smell of the sea was everywhere. It was in the warehouses that stored the cargoes. It was in the sail makers' yards and in the clothes of people working down by the river and on the docks, even the taverns where ships crews quenched their thirst smelt of the sea and the sound of their laughter filled the air.

Denison Street, Waterloo Road at the bottom end

Kitty's House (on left) in Denison Street. Demolished in 1951

Every few yards that Kitty walked in seeking employment a changing odour would seep from the many warehouses along the way, filling the air with pleasant, foul and sickly smells. The shops too had their own distinctive smells as most goods would be on open display. Fresh bread baked on the premises, sides of beef and other meat would be hanging from hooks, fresh from a local slaughter house. The smell of coffee, rice and other pleasant foods competed with the ale in the taverns, of which there were many, had their own aroma to tempt people.

Kitty did not leave Low Mill with a purse full of money   that would enable her to keep a roof over her head for a few weeks. The little she earned in her last three years at the mill only just about paid for her lodgings in the village. Kitty had to find some sort of employment, for she knew the spectre of the workhouse towered above those without means.

Because she had the ability to present herself in the most effective way. it was not long before she found employment. Kitty soon found employment with a Colonel Maxwell's family as a domestic servant. Mrs Maxwell had taken a liking to Kitty after speaking to people who attended the same Church as Kitty and spoke highly of her. Kitty was very happy in her new job, no longer did she have to suffer the long hours and the noise of the machines at Low Mill.

Although Kitty had to work hard as a domestic servant, this did not bother her. At last she was in control of her own destiny. When she was not on duty Kitty was getting to know the town, and she was making friends while attending the services at her local Unitarian Church. It is almost certain Kitty would have had to sit on wooden benches at the rear of the church reserved for poor people in the community. However Kitty would have been noticed attending church services by those in a position of privilege in the town. Kitty at twenty-one was a confident and proud young woman who would hold her head high, bringing those around to notice her.

The Maxwells proved to be good employers to Kitty, but after just one year in their employment the Maxwells had to leave Liverpool. Before they left, Mrs. Maxwell tried to persuade Kitty to go with them, but to no avail, she was not prepared to leave her mother. Because of her ability and good work record, it was not long before Kitty once again found employment with the family of Mrs. Richard Heywood, again as a domestic servant. This new post lasted for three years, by this time Kitty was twenty-five when her employment terminated.

Herbert R. Rathbone describes Kitty's working conditions during the time she was with the Heywood's when he wrote:

> *In this post she had a mistress who, by her own activity and exactness, and the vigilant observation which she exercised over the work of each servant, gave a very good training to all under her care. Kitty had the good sense to see that whatever knowledge she could gain beyond the immediate line of her own duties could become valuable to her in the future. She was always ready and willing to assist her fellow servants, in order that she might learn all branches of household work. This disposition to learn, joined with a habit of exact observation, enabled her to lay up a large store of useful knowledge which later proved invaluable to her and others.*

Kitty could no longer leave her mother on her own during the day. In order to maintain herself, Kitty opened a school. This would enable Kitty to have her mother with her during lessons and see to her needs.

Kitty did not need any teaching experience, the main considerations were premises and an ability to read and write. In those days a licence was not needed to start a school, compulsory education was still a long way off. This state of affairs unfortunately attracted unscrupulous people who had little or no interest in the welfare of the children, their main aim was to make money from the venture. However, whilst Kitty needed to make a living for her mother and herself the welfare of the children came first. She had seen how children were treated in the mills and that left a profound effect on Kitty. She managed to obtain a large room which served as her home and school for five pounds a year rent.

In one corner of the room Kitty had a bed for herself and her mother, the rest of the space was taken up by pupils during the day. The number attending classes each day could be from ten up to ninety children who sat on the bare floor. Those numbers may seem excessive, so many children in one room, but if you were poor you had little choice which went for Kitty as well as her pupils.

Those in better circumstances in the town rented the basements to as many as twenty or thirty people, without cooking facilities or water . In praising Kitty, Winefride R. Rathbone wrote:

If we try to imagine what Kitty's first impressions of Liverpool were, we shall probably come to the conclusion that the chief one was dirt. She had to make her new home in a grimy little back street, which looked as though it had never had a bath in its life. Inside her home, indeed, things were better; she could scrub and scour and polish and dust.

Winefride R. Rathbone went on to describe the scene outside of the house when she wrote:

But when she went out - poor Kitty! She could scarcely breathe in the bad air, and the sights she saw filled her heart with horror and pity. Hundreds of people men, women and little children, were then living in dark, damp cellars, in places were nowadays no one would allow even a dog to be kept. Some of those cellars, belonged to the rich people, who lived comfortably in the big house above.

Kitty charged her scholars three pence a week. She taught them reading writing and sewing, while her mother employed herself in making lace. At night when the school day was over, Kitty would go out and sell the items of lace her mother had made. Although the school was a success, life for Kitty and her mother was still very hard and at times it was difficult for them to afford food for themselves. No matter how bad things were for Kitty she retained a very happy disposition and always transmitted that happiness to her pupils. She was a ray of hope and inspired her young charges.

The health of her mother was still a great worry to Kitty and as the months went by her mother became more of a problem. She was starting to cause problems for Kitty during the times when her pupils were in class. Whenever Kitty was away from their home, her mother would sometimes burn their store of food or destroy valuables and bedding. The neighbours would intervene in Kitty's absence, to stop her mother from hurting herself.

In the middle of the night Mrs. Seaward would sometimes wander away to another part of the town where she had formerly lived. Her increasing violence frightened the children and caused Kitty to give up her school which was a bitter blow. The life she wanted most, was to be in her little school passing on skills she had learned during childhood.

The school was closed, but Kitty still had to make a living, rent still had to be paid. It was not possible for her to go back into domestic work because of the condition of her mother. Kitty was prepared to do almost anything to keep a roof over their heads. She would not allow her pride to get in the way of earning money no matter how menial.

It was not unusual to see people in those days shovelling horse manure into buckets from the streets to be sold to farmers. The countryside being so close to the town, also drew people into fields and country lanes to collect horse and cattle manure. Kitty, like so many desperate people in those days, would arise from her bed at two o'clock in the morning to go out into the country. Armed with her bucket and shovel, she would spend hours collecting the manure, then would deposit this in a hole in a field for safe keeping, to be sold to a local farmer later in the day.

Kitty had to give up the room she rented, and acquired a place to live in the countryside away from the stench of the town. She had hoped the fresh air would be good for her mother's health. However Kitty's employment prospects did not improve, so they returned to town.

This time the Seawards were successful in finding accommodation in Denison Street, although it was only a cellar. This was the place Kitty's mother often wandered back to. Kitty hoped by going to live there, her mother might become more settled. In the cellar next door there lived an elderly woman who was alone. She was a former friend of Mrs. Seaward. Kitty had often visited the woman in her cellar, which resembled a dungeon rather than a home. Several of Kitty's old scholars followed to her new home, but the cellar was so small she could only accommodate a few children. To supplement her small income she would work muslin for the shops, a plain-weave cotton fabric.

The hard work was taking its toll on Kitty and her youth was quickly passing by. Then, at the age of twenty-seven, she met Emanuel Demontee, a French Catholic seaman. How Kitty came to meet Emanuel Demontee we may never be sure. However just across the road from Denison Street was the Borough Gaol, known as the French Prison. This was the main holding centre for French prisoners of war in Liverpool and during 1800-1801, Dr

Marriage certificate of Kitty Seaward and Emanuel Demontee

Marriage certificate of Kitty and Emanuel
in the presence of a witness.

James Currie became very concerned for the welfare of the French prisoners. Many had died through overcrowding and the poor quality of the small amount of food allocated to them each week.

Other leading members of Liverpool's society took up the cause of the prisoners and agreement was reached with the French Government, that the Prisoners of war would be allowed to work in the community. In this way they would be able to feed and clothe themselves much better. It is possible that Emanuel Demontee was one of those prisoners of war and Kitty met him whilst working in the community.

They were married in the Parish Church of St. Peter, Liverpool, on the 5th October, 1812. An observer at the time of the marriage commenting on the character of Demontee said: "By all accounts he was a very respectable man, and a kind and affectionate husband, and he agreed to Kitty's stipulations, that she was never to be asked to change her religion or the place of her worship, and her children if any, were to be brought up as Protestants." 1812 was not a popular time to be a Catholic, yet Kitty chose to marry Emanuel Demontee. This was long before Catholic Emancipation in 1829.

In 1813 Kitty gave birth to her first child, a son, whom she called John. At the time of the birth, Emanuel Demontee is reported to have been at sea in the merchant service. Kitty had a second son when she was in her thirties. At the time of her confinement Demontee was again away from home in the merchant service. Later he was reported to have been drowned at sea before the birth of his second son. Herbert R. Rathbone in his edited memoir wrote:

> *Emanuel Demontee was absent in Canada when he heard of his wife's approaching confinement and he immediately sold all he possessed in order that he might send money to assist her.*

He set sail for home but tragically the ship on which he was sailing foundered and all hands perished. There is no explanation of how Demontee discovered his wife's 'impending confinement,' it would have been almost impossible for an articled seaman to receive a message. Could it have been that Emanuel Demontee, was intending to settle in Canada? Being a Frenchman, Emanuel Demontee would not have felt out of place in the Province of Quebec. It is also possible that he was on his way to Liverpool after preparing the ground for his family, for a new life in Canada? Kitty would have been a blessing to any man wanting to emigrate to the new world.

5

The Young Widow
1815-1831

The young widow with two young children and an ailing mother to care for and her youngest child in poor health, was now trapped in a sea of misery once again having to face the fear of poverty. Her friends urged her to place her mother in an asylum, but Kitty was not prepared to turn her back on her mother. Although Kitty had what seemed insurmountable problems, she had also concerned herself in trying to keep orphan children from the community out of the workhouse.

Kitty may have been trapped, living in cellars in the most appalling conditions; but her spirit was indomitable. She carried on fighting for her very existence, and yet, she still had time for other people. Midwives were unknown at this time and medical facilities in general were very poor. However Kitty was earning a reputation for attending the sick in her area. Despite her ability to look after other people Kitty was forced to take whatever work came her way. She could not enter domestic service because of her children and her mother. Kitty needed work that would allow her to be home during the midday break and to finish work at a reasonable hour in the evening. She found employment in a nail factory close to her home which enabled her to see to her children and mother during the midday break.

Kitty Wilkinson

The work was hard and the wages small, Kitty got three pence for every twelve hundred nails she produced. The average wage that could be earned was four shillings a week, but at times she actually managed to earn as much as eight shillings. Kitty paid the price for her hard work, her fingers were continually burned with the heat of the nails. This was brought about by removing the nails from under a heavy power hammer after stamping. When her hands were too blistered and sore, she would have to stay at home without pay and dress them until they healed again. After enduring this hard labour for more than a year she was forced to give up, in order to keep her sanity and general health.

There were four nail manufacturers in business in Liverpool where she could have worked. They were all within walking distance of her home. They were T. Gibbons, 6 Beckwith Street; Jas Hatton, 11 Freemasons Row, Wm. Hazard, 2 Norfolk Street and John Price, 26 Ray Street. The manufacturer Jas Hatton was close to Denison Street.

Not long after giving up this soul-destroying job, Kitty, proud and strong as she most certainly was, was forced to apply to the parish for help in the maintenance of her two children and mother. The fact that she was born in Ireland which was in union with the United Kingdom at that time, made Kitty doubt her claim to relief. Her claim was admitted, and for a short time she was given two shillings a week for her children.

Once again she was obliged to work collecting manure, ready to sell to local farmers, and doing part-time domestic work, or anything else that she could do to look after her family. She knew only too well that her own strength and strong character were the only weapons she possessed to keep the doors of the workhouse at a distance. Standing like a vulture at the top of Brownlow Hill, was the spectre of the Workhouse which hung over Kitty and the rest of her community.

Thousands of poor people within the areas of Leeds Street, in the north of the town, stretching to Parliament Street in the south of Liverpool, lived in daily fear of sickness or unemployment. The only alternative for people who were unemployed or homeless was the workhouse, and after admittance they would be classed as paupers.

The Brownlow Hill Workhouse was one of the biggest in the country, at times with over 3,500 people incarcerated in return for their accommodation. The inmates had to work all day in the most appalling conditions, for which they received food that was little better than pig swill. The sick and the vagrant all mixed together, sleeping in vastly overcrowded rooms, spreading disease often resulting in plague. Almost fifty years later things were just as bad for those unfortunate enough to be admitted to the workhouse.

Writing on the 4th February 1867, Agnes Jones, who was the first trained nurse to enter the workhouse wrote:

I sometimes wonder if there is a worse place on earth, but I never regret coming and I never wish to give it up.

This wonderful and devoted nurse, who was so concerned with the plight of the poor, was dead by the age of thirty-four. She contracted typhoid nursing the sick in the workhouse hospital.

A steady stream of people were going to Kitty most days for help mostly in a practical way. However she was not always able to keep the spectre of the workhouse door from all of them. It was for the children that Kitty was most concerned as she knew from her own experience what lay in store for them in servitude in the dark satanic mills. There would be times when Kitty felt the pain of seeing children and parents entering the workhouse, knowing that she, or anybody else, could not do anything to stop this happening.

Kitty Wilkinson

Meanwhile Kitty was still going out charring, and when offered food to eat during the day Kitty would ask if she could take it home with her to eat later. However her employers knew only too well why she did this, it was so she could share it with her mother and children. Such was the poverty of Kitty's household, during this time. One or two friends from the Church she attended would give her the flowers from their gardens, which Kitty sold on a Saturday to buy extra food.

It would be very easy to feel Kitty's life was one of sheer gloom, but this was far from the truth. Kitty was very happy and had a cheerful disposition. It was during this period in her life that she started to do some domestic work for a family, Mr. and Mrs. Alexander Braik, trading as Dye's at 6 Pit Street. Whenever they were busy and needed extra help they would call in Kitty. The Braik family were practising Methodists and very caring people who had adopted an orphan girl. At meal times Mr. and Mrs. Braik, together with their children, would have meals with the servants. They were known to say that: "Our Lord always ate with His disciples."

Kitty, despite all her problems in looking after her own family and neighbours, was also drawn into helping Mrs. Braik in her charitable work. Whenever Kitty came across a family in need she would let Mrs. Braik know of their circumstances, and Mrs. Braik would pay them a visit. She would also visit the sick, read to them, say some prayers and, before leaving, leave some money, wrapped in paper for them.

Mrs. Braik would sometimes say to Kitty, after one of her visits to the poor:

Thou hast given me a great pleasure by telling me of such and such a one; she wants such and such things; thou must help me to make them, and that will be thy mite.

During the last eighteen months of her life Mrs. Braik was a sick woman, and although Kitty nursed her, Kitty was also expected to visit the sick on her behalf. All this extra work meant that Kitty had to engage someone to look after her mother and children while she herself was absent.

Although Mr. and Mrs. Braik were well meaning people the payment Kitty got from her employer was hardly enough to feed her family and keep a roof over their heads. Kitty must have felt very frustrated at times being the intelligent woman that she was; knowing she had the skills to give her a better standard of living. However in order to improve her own position in life, she would have had to leave her family to fend for themselves and this she was not prepared to do.

During the last days of her life Mrs. Braik said to Kitty: "May thy last days be thy best days." However it would be a long time before Kitty would see her best days. Mrs. Braik never forgot Kitty. She left instructions that after her death, her husband should continue to befriend Kitty, which he dutifully did by giving her a mangle and plenty of work. Having a mangle may not seem much by today's standards, but at that time it would be similar to receiving a washing machine. This act enabled Kitty to earn a living and to work more efficiently. But still, the extra work given to her by Mr. Blaik did not keep hunger entirely from her door. Kitty was well known for feeding her family first and whoever else that might be living under her roof at the time.

Like many women in her position she allowed her own health to suffer while caring for others. Kitty's youngest son was causing his mother great concern as his health deteriorated, his illness being such that he could not lie down in bed. Kitty had to sit up with him for many weeks, even after a hard day's work. The young man was kept alive through the attention and devotion of his mother.

Kitty Wilkinson

The hard work and sober habits of Kitty started to pay off and she was able to rent a small house in Denison Street. Her Unitarian friends both rich and poor were delighted for her but they knew she would use her extra accommodation to help others worse off than herself. A poor widow by the name of Mary Powell, who had been a friend of Kitty's mother, was dismissed from the workhouse sometime in 1818. The woman had no place to live and Kitty seeing her in such a destitute condition, took her into her own home. The woman was deaf and gradually became blind, but for the first eighteen months living with Kitty, Mary Powell was able to earn a little towards her keep.

Once again the tide changed in favour of Kitty as she started to reach middle age. Ten years had passed since her husband died leaving her with two children and a handicapped mother to look after. Kitty was thirty-eight when a new man came into her life, He was Thomas Wilkinson. Winefride R. Rathbone in her memoir of Kitty wrote:

> *Perhaps you will remember the name of Thomas Wilkinson, the boy she had known in the long-ago days when she was a little girl working in the cotton mill at Caton. He had not forgotten Kitty, and there is a pretty story of how they met one another again in the grimy Liverpool streets. It was through the old Lancashire songs that Kitty had learned as a village child, and which she still sang as a woman in her dark town dwelling. Perhaps he too was feeling lonely and sad when, one day when he was walking through the streets, he suddenly heard someone singing the old songs he remembered so well.*

Thomas Wilkinson was employed as a porter in Mr. William Rathbone's cotton warehouse in Liverpool. Mr. Rathbone was a prominent member of the Unitarian church. After a short courtship Thomas and Kitty were married. Their wedding took place at Holy Trinity Church in Liverpool on the 1st December 1823. He was unable to read or write, so his name was entered for him, followed by his mark. Kitty signed her own name Catherine Demontee, the witnesses to the marriage were William Fisher and Mary Powell.

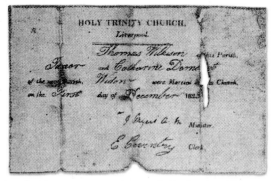

Marriage certificate showing signature of Catherine and mark of Thomas

Certificate showing marriage of Catherine Demontee and Thomas Wilkinson, December 1, 1823

Kitty Wilkinson

Thomas was nine years younger, than Kitty it would seem unlikely they would have been friends at Caton Mill. Kitty was eighteen when she left the apprentice house to live in the village of Caton. Thomas, at the end of each working day would have been taken back to the apprentice house, so the chance of any contact between him and Kitty would have been very remote.

Thomas was living in Frederick Street when he met Kitty. This was the street Kitty lived in for a short while on her return from Caton. In all probability Kitty and Thomas would have known one another from living in Frederick Street and from being members of the same Church. An article in the Liverpool Mercury of May, 1932, reported that a Thomas Wilkinson was a gardener who lived in Frederick Street, and worked in Greenbank Road for William Rathbone. It is also recorded that Thomas was a gardener and a Unitarian when he married Kitty.

Thomas was regarded as a good and honest man with qualities similar to those of Kitty. He was more than willing to share in the responsibility of looking after Kitty's mother and the two children. He was also prepared to take on the burden of attending to Mary Powell, who continued to live with the Wilkinsons. Mary Powell in time became completely dependent on the Wilkinsons. Kitty continued to nurse her for many years, even though she had her own mother and children to care for.

A few weeks after they were married, Mrs. Jones a neighbour, asked Kitty if she could attend to one of her children who had taken ill and this she did. Kitty did not know Mrs. Jones very well but shortly after, she also attended the woman herself who had become very ill. Sadly Mrs. Jones never recovered from her illness and died a couple of weeks later. She left four children and no relations to look after them. Kitty spoke to Thomas about the situation and he agreed they should take the children. He said he would be prepared to cut down on food himself if need be, and also work longer hours. They accepted responsibility for the four children, and looked after them as though they were their own.

The eldest was a girl, who later married, and the second girl turned out to be a great help to Kitty in the house. The other two children were boys, the eldest eventually went to sea and the second boy went into the Blue Coat School, which took in orphan children and gave them an education.

Shortly after accepting responsibility for Mrs Jones' children, Kitty and Thomas took in two more orphan boys. They were not very strong, but with love and care the Wilkinsons soon nursed them back to health. The boys were later apprenticed and were employed by a Captain Finley who was a friend of Kitty and Thomas. He owned his own ship and was prepared to take charge of orphans who were not afraid of hard work. Captain Finley lost his life, being washed over board from his ship in a heavy storm.

The sea was the major means of employment for Liverpool men. Becoming a seaman would seem be a natural thing for a boy to want to do. There was a great loss of life at sea in those days as ships were only a fraction of the size they are now and far less stable and at the mercy of the elements to a much greater extent than today. A couple of years after Thomas's marriage to Kitty they had managed to save some money, and were persuaded by a Patrick Dunn to move into a larger house.

Patrick Dunn was a widower with three small children, who was in full time employment and agreed to pay twenty-four shillings a week for board and lodgings for himself and his children. Patrick was a Roman Catholic, but his late wife had been a Protestant and he promised her the children should be brought up in her faith. After her death he took the children regularly to his wife's church to honour his promise. He lived with the Wilkinson's for seven years and he worked in a foundry until the end of his life. Because Patrick Dunn was a Roman Catholic, Kitty always provided him with fish on Fridays, and observed the rituals that his religion demanded of him. Her final act of kindness to him was to send for a priest, when she realised he was dying. Kitty is reported to have said: *"People go fastest to heaven their own way."*

So once again the Wilkinsons had three more orphans to look after, the youngest boy went into the Bluecoat School and finished up as a seaman. The girl whose name was Betsy went into service and was later to marry Kitty's own son John Demontee. The eldest boy was apprenticed at sea, but was unsuited to this pursuit. As they did not want him to become a labourer, they found a place for him in the drawing-school of the Mechanic's Institute in order to improve his chances in the trade of carver and gilder.

Thomas and Kitty continued to take orphans and other homeless people into their home for years to come. Whenever it was possible they would send the children to the Bluecoat School to be educated. Thomas knew the value of education no matter how limited, having himself been denied a basic education. This was, perhaps, why he placed such a high value on education for children in their care. It is a sad reflection on society that then, as now, in spite of all the good work Kitty and her husband did in their community their contribution was not fully appreciated by their contemporaries.

In another example of the demands made on Kitty and her husband, Herbert R. Rathbone, wrote:

In the year 1827, Mrs. Wilkinson was called out to a Mr. Christian, man in the last stage of consumption. After a life spent in ignorance and neglect of religion, he was now, for the first time, awakening to a sense of its awful importance. His wife and family continued in so hardened a state of insensibility that his dying exhortations and entreaties were unheeded by them, and had no power to undo the effects of his past indifference and bad example. Their Sabbaths were between labour and amusements, and they entirely neglected all the duties of religion.

Great store was put on people attending Church and carrying out their religious duties, even though many poor people were living in the most vile conditions. Rathbone also wrote,

The children had never been baptised; but this rite Mrs Wilkinson induced the parents to have performed, and she stood godmother to them all. The conduct of the mother, however, put it out of her power to fulfil the duties she had thus taken upon herself.

After the death of Mr. Christian, Kitty was said to have lent her mangle to his widow, to enable her to support her family on the condition that if she should become the more needy of the two, it was to be returned. During the seven years of Mrs Christian's remaining life, for the last three of which she appeared to be dying of consumption, Kitty continued her kind offices, though they were but too frequently returned by abuse.

When Mrs. Christian died, Kitty offered to divide her own clothes with the eldest girl if she would go into domestic service. She was also willing to take the two boys into her own house, although what they earned could not maintain them. Kitty was also prepared to get the youngest girl into the Bluecoat School; but they rejected her offers. The young parentless family moved to another neighbourhood. Some time afterwards, hearing they had fallen into difficulties living on their own, Kitty sent food parcels and asked other friends to help.

Kitty heard Mrs. Christian's eldest son Tom was dying. She sent for him immediately, and had him brought to her own house, and nursed him till he died. For the last month of his life, he required attention day and night, and she sat up with him every night during that period. Kitty said at the time of his death:

Kitty Wilkinson

He suffered much, but gave every proof of sincere repentance and expressed great anxiety about his former associates.

Kitty spoke to the minister who was to officiate at the funeral, as to the life style of the deceased and the circumstances of the case, so he might take the opportunity of addressing those assembled. She then invited a number of his former companions to attend his funeral. Kitty hoped that what the minister was about to preach, would be to the lasting good of many present. After his death, she got his youngest sister admitted into the Bluecoat School, and took the other boy to live with her. The Bluecoat School was providing the education for some of Kitty's bright children. Kitty's concern for the education of working class children in her community was still of great importance to her.

By 1828, Kitty and Thomas were still looking after Kitty's mother, who must have been a great age by now, Kitty herself was in her mid-forties which would in itself be considered a great age at that time. The mother's health was causing Kitty and Thomas some distress, but they continued to look after her rather than have her committed to the workhouse. Hospitals were non-existent and medication was not much beyond the primitive stage.

During the constant worry of her mother, Kitty had to look after her second son, who had been in poor health from the day he was born. His life however was drawing to a close and after his death Kitty considered it a merciful release. She was unable to sleep and could not eat food for some time after he died. However, with so much sickness in her community people were still knocking on her door. They were desperate especially those living in the cellars without running water, making it difficult for people to look after themselves. The Courts that Kitty had watched being built alongside Denison Street over the years, were not much better than the cellars. The only water supplied was just one standpipe in the courtyard to serve many households.

By 1830 the commerce of the town was thriving and the rich continued to abandon residing in the town. Living in the gentle pastures of the countryside was more conducive to their life style. As wealthy merchants moved out, the poor were still pouring in to the town looking for work. However there were a few merchants with genuine concern for the plight of the poor working people of the town, especially those who had come to know Kitty. By 1832 Liverpool was still a very small borough, bound by the Mersey, Boundary Street in the north and Parliament Street in the south.

Kitty Wilkinson

6

Cholera
1832

At the start of the New Year of 1832 a notable event took place in the lives of the Liverpool merchant class; a visit from the musical prodigy, Nicolo Paganini, the great Italian violinist. He gave three concerts at the beginning of January in the Theatre Royal, Williamson Square, and three others subsequently. However his reputation for high admission charges caused much comment by many Liverpool ladies who donated much of their time to charitable work. Their concern was that the lowest price in the gallery was five shillings. Paganini did, however, make some amends by donating his services at a concert on January 30th for the relief of the poor.

The 'New Year' as with other New Years before, did not start well for thousands of poor in the town. Apart from the little charity coming from middle class ladies, little or no relief came to the poor from any other quarter. Poor children, many of them in bare feet, had no alternative but to play in dirty cold streets. A warm January day would be a luxury but cold days also had the single advantage at least, of keeping some germs at bay.

Kitty and her husband Thomas Wilkinson were still living in Denison Street involved in helping their community. Kitty continued to be called upon to nurse the sick and when she was not nursing took in orphans from the street.

The houses in Denison Street had been well constructed in 1780. At the top end the street joined off Great Howard Street and the lower end of it came out onto Bath Street. Denison Street housed the middle class and trades people of the area until about 1810. To the north side of Denison Street lay green fields and open land with small hamlets in the distance. The countryside was filled with wild life, stretched for miles down river towards the small township of Bootle along the Lancashire coast.

After 1810, the "dreaded" courts were in the course of being built alongside Denison Street. They were as close to each other as possible to extract the maximum amount of money from the large numbers of people who could be crammed into them. The population started to increase as new people moved into the area, slowly at first but gradually gaining in momentum. As the new docks moved further down river towards Kirkdale, the dock masters were requiring more labour to load and unload ships. The shipping using the river was increasing year by year and Liverpool became the highway to the 'New World' of America. The green fields were fast disappearing, as more docks and warehouses were built on both sides of the town. Where once there were sandy beaches, walls of granite appeared along the shore-line.

Workers for the new docks and warehouses needed to be housed as near to their place of work as possible. During the time the courts were being built, people were still moving in to cellars throughout Liverpool, the majority of these cellars had three or four families living in them. The courts were constructed in the shape of a horseshoe, with the entrance through a narrow passage. On each side of a court, (which were built back to back) there were four or five houses each with three small rooms.

The courtyards were approximately nine to fifteen feet wide, and each had a further court attached to it. The houses themselves had very little ventilation and refuse was collected on an ad hoc irregular basis. Facing the entrance were the privies (toilets) constructed without running water.

There were usually only two, or at most three, privies serving a Court which had to cater for as many as twenty families constantly using them, some of the privies even had doors missing. At irregular intervals the contents of the privy would be removed sometimes after it had been full for days.

Very little sunshine penetrated the houses due to the narrowness of the courts, and the only way people could get fresh air was by standing outside in the courtyard. People had little choice between the smell inside the house and the stench outside. A single stand pipe, in each courtyard was the only way to obtain water. It is recorded that the water supply was turned on once or twice a day, according to some reports it was only on alternate days.

When the water did come on, it would be erratically timed i.e. six o'clock in the morning, or even eleven o'clock at night. Sometimes people would have to stand waiting in all weathers long before the water was turned on. They would then fill up pots and pans hoping to have sufficient to carry them over until the next water supply time. People living in cellars had little chance to store water. The space they occupied would not allow for storage and their possessions would be so small many would not have the correct utensils for storage.

The water supply in Liverpool was in the hands of private water companies who felt they had the right to deny people in the poorer districts a water supply, which would help ensure them a basic right to life.

Houses in Denison Street all had running water, so it would seem that the water companies would have had little difficulty in supplying water to the courts which were adjacent to the Street.

Kitty Wilkinson

Kitty's involvement in her community was known to other members of her church and those who had a more comfortable life style tried to help where they could.

Although Kitty was not a member of the privileged class she had come to the notice of William Rathbone and his wife Elizabeth. Mrs. Rathbone with one or two other ladies gave the lead in encouraging other women of her class to combine in helping the poor. However well meaning the efforts of these women, they could not change the minds of those who controlled the water supply to the town, or the private landlords who built slum housing.

As the winter of 1832 was giving way to the onset of spring, news was beginning to filter through that all was not well in the poorer districts of Europe. Cholera had been reported in many areas and by April the first sign of cholera was evident in Liverpool. Great panic had spread throughout Liverpool and it was not only the poor who feared for their lives, but also many of the middle-class who worked and lived alongside the poor.

With the help of her husband Thomas, Kitty worked day and night to try and combat the nightmare that had erupted all around them. The signs of what was to come must have been all too clear to Kitty, for she had been actively involved with those who were homeless and sick for most of her life. The fact that Kitty was living in Denison Street before the outbreak of cholera seems to show her lot in life was a little better than most, yet her concern was always for those who were worse off.

Kitty had access to running water and more comforts than most of the neighbours so the combination of water and Kitty's humanity were the catalyst of her life-saving efforts on behalf of her neighbours. She was a true Christian, one who had time for those less well off than herself and a devout member of her church. She would help anybody, no matter who they were, or what religion they practised. Being in need was the only qualification that mattered to her. Kitty attempted to combat the cholera by using clean hot water, which she had brought to a boiling point in the large boiler she had installed in her cellar and she actively encouraged her neighbours to wash their bedding and clothes. Cholera is an acute infectious disease and infection usually occurs from drinking contaminated water. The first abrupt symptom is profuse diarrhoea, often accompanied by vomiting. This may lead to rapid loss of fluid and salts, causing muscle cramps, severe thirst and cold, wrinkled skin. If lost fluids are not replaced, coma and death may follow within twenty-four hours.

The cholera hung like a thick black cloud over the town and people had no place to turn from the terror which haunted them. This was a challenge that had to be met, and Kitty took it up at a time when there seemed to be little or no hope. At the height of the cholera epidemic Kitty did not run, as many others had done. She stayed and went among her panic-stricken neighbours. She kept calm wherever she went, trying to raise the hopes of all she came in contact with. Kitty, with the full backing of her husband, went into the homes of the sick and dying, to bring not only comfort and advice, but also clean bedding.

Kitty nursed the sick, at a time when others were afraid to go anywhere near them for fear of infection. However by her example she encouraged other women to follow her lead. Somehow, whether by some divine providence or natural ability Kitty was able to convince people that cleanliness and fresh air was a major part of the answer to combating cholera. Kitty nursed the sick and gave good advice, but that advice was not always welcome. Often people could not see the connection when told about washing their bedding and clothing, when they were living in such poor homes without water.

The first death occurred on May 4 in Denison Street, a Mr.

Tolson a widower with two children. Mrs. Mac Allister with whom he lodged tried to attend to him, but in desperation she called on Kitty as the doctors were unable to cope with the demands put upon them. After the death of the man, Kitty was directed by a physician not to allow anyone to wash the corpse. When the local people heard about the corpse not being washed, a crowd assembled outside the house behaving in a riotous manner. The assembled crowd where insisting the body should not be buried unwashed. It was some time before the crowd would listen to anything Kitty tried to say. She addressed the excited people in a quiet manner.

We are sorry if you feel that we have done anything wrong, Mrs. Mac Allister and myself have tried to do our best, and what is right. But if any of you will wash the body, we will find you everything necessary.

The crowd silently dispersed, and the body was buried unwashed. This was the start of the disease that raged with great violence for many weeks in one of the most closely populated and poorest districts of the town. Kitty first went to the doctors for advice, then reported back to them on the progress of the patients. Apart from Kitty's helpers such as her husband Thomas, most of the doctors kept a safe distance from the cholera victims. Kitty and her husband shared their own food, sheets and blankets with the sick.

In the Port of Liverpool the 'Brutus' an emigrant ship took on board passengers who were hoping to start a new life in Canada. She left the port for Quebec on May 18th 1832 with 330 passengers; on May 28th cholera broke out on board. Many of the crew where affected and conditions on board had become so bad the Captain had no option but to turn back to Liverpool. The ship arrived back on June 14th but by then ninety-seven deaths had taken place.

Kitty attracted the attention of some benevolent people and, among the things they supplied was oatmeal, which enabled her to make porridge for those in desperate need. There would be occasions when Kitty would be looking after as many as sixty people - men, women and children. One of Thomas's jobs was to bring home as much milk as he could carry every night after his day's work.

Kitty would often spread bedding on the floor of a vacant room to accommodate families whilst their own homes were being disinfected. Many children were homeless, some without parents because of the cholera and Kitty had the extra burden of trying to house them.

Until this disaster Kitty was unknown to people outside her own community. The local media in general was unconcerned about the plight of the poor. However, her work came to the notice of the District Provident Society who gave her much needed help by providing bedding and used clothes.

Kitty worked long hours, always putting the needs of the sick and suffering people before herself and her husband. She was, at that time, recovering from an illness herself, and had been warned she would be putting her life in danger if she continued working such long hours, but, she still went ahead fulfilling what she felt to be her duty.

Many families were living in a single room without bedding or any of the creature comforts one would normally expect to find even for those times. This was the nightmare that had engulfed Kitty. However, she devoted all her time, thoughts, and all she possessed in an endeavor to lessen the misery around her. The few doctors on hand could not possibly cope. This was a time before nurses were available so she administered the remedies on the doctors' instructions.

Kitty set up a washroom in her kitchen, boiling water in a large copper container in the corner of the room. Then she got Thomas to fix up clotheslines in the yard. Kitty then invited her poorer neighbours who were without the means of boiling water to wash the infected clothes and bedding. The newly washed garments and bedding could be seen drying in the yard night and day.

Another reason for Kitty encouraging people to dry their clothes in her yard, was to make sure their clothes were dried properly. People would often put on damp clothes, not having the proper facilities for drying. This lead by Kitty was probably the turning point in letting people know they should have the right to clean water and better sanitary conditions.

By the autumn of the year 5,000 people had been affected, more than 1,500 people died out of a population of 230,000. The great supporters of Kitty in her praiseworthy efforts were Mr. and Mrs. Rathbone who were already aware of her concern for the poor. She also received great help from Rector Campbell and members of the congregation of her church.

The District Provident Society got to know of Kitty's methods in tackling the cholera outbreak. They gave her help she needed in providing soap and other assistance, for washing cholera infected clothes and bedding. A local Surgeon also called to see Kitty to give her some advice on how infected clothes and bedding might, by the help of chloride of lime, be washed without risk to those engaged in doing it. Kitty was giving the lead in her neighbourhood showing the wider community how to tackle this menace, that was taking its toll. Poor people in other parts of Liverpool were having clothes and bedding burned by order of the magistrates. Such was the lack of understanding of cholera and its treatment.

Even the medical profession was uncertain as to the causes of cholera and many papers were written by eminent practitioners as to its cause. One such paper was by W.W Squiries M.D.,

Honorary Physician to the Liverpool Cholera Hospital.

In laying before my professional brethren the results of my experience in more than 1,200 cases of cholera, I feel considerable diffidence, and claim their indulgence for whatever may appear imperfect. The opinions I shall advance will be given in a spirit of candour and free from intentional offence; not with a desire to decry the views or practice of others, but as an endeavour to justify my own.

After a lengthy description of the symptoms he goes on to describe what is thought to be the causes of cholera.

There is a serious difference of opinion as to the great and primary cause and the question "Is cholera contagious?" is not likely to be decided to the satisfaction of all parties. I might therefore avoid saying anything on this subject. I understand, that when a disease is called contagious or infectious, we speak of a certain distinguishing and pre-eminent quality. And I feel bound to state, that the inquiries I made into several hundred cases, for the purpose of settling this point and the unusually valuable opportunities I have had for observation, do not warrant the belief of its contagious nature.

Although the grand cause is involved in mystery, we may, presume the existence of a powerful morbific agent, which predisposition and various exciting causes call into action. These are, intemperance and irregular habits, over loading the stomach, poor, unwholesome and indigestible food, unripe fruits and the colder vegetables, such as cucumbers, wet feet, exposure to night air, cold and damp, or great heat, uncleanliness, ill-ventilated dwellings and impure air, fear and the depressing passions. In short, anything which disorders the nervous and circulating systems.

Kitty Wilkinson

In the many causes put forward by Squiries he mentions uncleanliness and ill-vented dwellings. However he does not appear to see them as some of the main cause of cholera, caused by foul living conditions forced on poor people. He gave other examples such as fear:

Many practitioners dispute the probability of Fear being capable of producing or exciting cholera. A woman who was in the habit of carrying a basket of earthenware for sale, when in perfect health and pursuing her avocation, arriving at the end of a street was met by an acquaintance who said, "Don't go into that street; you'll catch the cholera." The woman instantly set down the basket, ran home, and in three hours was brought to the hospital, at her own request, in the second stage of the complaint. She recovered. Another female, feeling no sign of indisposition, but whom apprehension had kept within doors, was visited by a friend, who said, "The cholera box is going past." The woman trembled, vomiting commenced and in a short time she was a corpse.

While all the debating was going on as to the causes of cholera Kitty was busy combatting the disease with clean water and disinfectant. Word soon spread that a washhouse had been started by Mrs Wilkinson in Denison Street. Kitty contrived to provide for the washing of, on average, eighty-five families per week. People contributed 'one penny per week' to assist in defraying expenses.

Herbert R. Rathbone wrote:

Another valuable institution for the neighbourhood also originated from Kitty's action at this time. During the prevalence of this dreadful disease, which principally seized on and carried off the heads of families, many children

whose parents were dead or dying, and who were too young
to be admitted into any of the schools (as there was then no
infant schools in the neighbourhood) were running about
the streets neglected.

Kitty collected about twenty orphaned children in her bedroom
and a neighbour, Mrs. Lloyd, began to teach them simple hymns
and stories and sing to them. The numbers increased and by
degrees an infant school was formed without funds or books or
chairs for the children to sit on. The help of a benevolent
individual, whose name was not known, gave assistance to Kitty
in the furtherance of her labour of love. Was that benevolent
individual Mr.William Rathbone? Further help was also given by
the Corporation and the result was a school for one hundred and
ninety children. Mrs. Lloyd was rewarded for her good work and
leadership, by her appointment as head mistress.

Liverpool Corporation at the time of the epidemic had not taken
any comprehensive responsibility to bring about a water supply
for everyone, although as far back as 1786 the council had the
powers to supply water. In 1794 the Corporation purchased from
a private concern some caravans that were based on the north
shore and spent £5,000 renovating them. In a marketing pamphlet
distributed amongst the genteel members of society in the town, it
described the benefits of the caravans:

As commodious, safe, elegant, as any of the kind in
England, and having all the advantages of the salubrity of
the salt water without exposing the bather to view.

A floating bath was also moored in the river, long before the
great influx of poor people into the town. It was housed on two
boats and was built so that a continuous supply of water filled the
bath. These facilities were not for the poor people of the town,
they knew their place and would never try to set foot on board. It

was not however unusual for even the upper and middle classes to bathe as infrequently as once a year. Kitty's efforts with the boiler in her cellar was really the beginning of the first public washhouse in the world and did an immense amount to combat the cholera epidemic locally. Winifred Rathbone, highlights the lack of support from the Corporation at that time:

> *There was absolutely no drainage, only a pit in the centre of the court yard or alley where all the refuse and rubbish was thrown and left to decay, making horrible smells, especially in the hot summer weather. And still the people crowded into this already crowded part of the town, and the more of them that there were the more dreadful it all became. The Corporation sent around carts sometimes to clear and clean the wider streets, but many of those courts were so narrow that no cart could get into them.*

Winifred Rathbone writes the poor people could have done more for themselves, but she could also see the massive problems people had with bad housing and lack of water. This was enough to make the strongest person give up hope, but her main criticism was levelled at the Corporation:

> *The Corporation seemed to think that this was not their business, and that they could not be expected to find any other way of cleaning them. So they left it to the inhabitants of the houses, who were, as a rule, too ignorant and lazy to do anything on their own account. It is difficult to imagine what these places must have been like.*

She could also understand the problems the poor had to endure through lack of water, controlled by the private water companies when she wrote:

> *It was not likely that people who lived in places like these would be very careful about keeping the inside of their*

houses very clean. However there is some excuse for them having no water supply inside of the houses and that every drop of it had to be carried in pails from a pipe outside.

The District Provident Society continued to try and ease the suffering of the poor, by providing some material things such as bedding. They also called from house-to-house, in an effort to encourage people to try and save some money they earned (a fruitless endeavor when you consider the very meager wages paid.) According to literature of the society, their aim was to:

Produce among the poor and the lower orders of the town and its vicinity habits of saving and economy. This important object it seeks to effect by employment of visitors to call on the poor at their own homes and receive from them weekly such deposits as they may be able to afford. The deposits are placed in the savings bank, bearing interest, and are payable to the depositors whenever they may require them.

Given the situation that most working people found themselves living in, the high ideals of the Society fell upon deaf ears, not entirely through choice but more through sheer practical necessity. During the winter months one of the main places of escape from the misery of their cellars and courts was to frequent the many taverns in the area. Denison Street, which had about thirty-five houses on each side and was no more than three hundred yards in length, had five taverns and two ale houses. They were The Pilot Boat, New York, Cross Keys, Grapes and Highlander Tavern and Star and Ship.

In No, 1 Denison Street lived a Mr. Edward Rowland who was described as a person who kept temperance rooms, he was warning people of the evils of alcohol and its effects being the work of the devil. However the devil had the upper hand, the

Kitty Wilkinson

taverns always had a warm fire in the grate, which was one way people, could keep warm during cold winter days. So people had the choice of a life of temperance with the chance of freezing to death in the cellars and courts, or they could choose a fire in the grate provided by the 'Inn Keeper.' The Inn also allowed people to commune with one another in a little comfort. The inn keeper of course was not so much concerned about the welfare of his customers, but the money he could extract from them.

> *The cholera carried on into the following year of 1833. With the onset of winter, Kitty was just as active in the service of her neighbours as she had been when the scourge first appeared. The earliest cases that came to her notice occurred in a cellar where a family of five and two neighbours who went to nurse them lay dead or dying. They all died within four days of one another.*

The neighbours of the victims pleaded with Kitty not to go in, and even tried to hold her back by force but she told them that people must not die for want of help. On one occasion Kitty was attending to a Mrs. Harrison, who was not known to her, and who died leaving five children. The deceased woman's husband was unemployed and Kitty suggested he should go to sea to earn money to support his children.

She readily agreed to look after the children. Unemployment was rife at this time, but a man stood a better chance finding employment as a seaman. In those days, the working and living conditions on board the small ships, in many cases, were dangerous, the death rate among seamen was high and also many ships were lost. When Kitty took charge of the children they had been neglected, but by the time their father arrived home from his voyage they were all in good health. Kitty proposed at this stage that a member of the man's family look after the children.

His sister agreed to look after them but sadly after some months had passed, Kitty's husband on his way to work saw the children playing in the street. All their good clothes had gone, and they begged him to take them back again. So Kitty once again agreed to take them into her care, where they remained until they reached adulthood.

The town council brought in new regulations governing the construction of cellars. This legislation demanded cellars had to have a minimum, headroom, which meant a great many of them were less than the standard legal height. In order to fulfil the statute, some owners decided just to dig out the floors and avoid the necessity of closing the cellars and losing rent. The Rev. Johns, stated:

The worst cellars that I am acquainted with are as bad and as densely inhabited as ever. In the catacombs of the living there is concealment without privacy; and we are yearly building new splendours over a buried social Pompeii, in which the ruins of decency are filled with the ashes of virtue.

Kitty Wilkinson

7

Vauxhall District

By 1835 life had changed very little for most people and the town was still receiving people looking for work. The new docks and factories were a magnet drawing people from all parts of the United Kingdom. No longer was Liverpool the tiny little town that opened its arms to Kitty in 1790.

The dreaded cholera was, however, still showing its ugly head although not to the same degree. Life for the people of Denison Street certainly had not changed for the better.

The Street was surrounded by the court system of housing. Great Howard Street at the top of Denison Street and Leeds Street, just the other side of Great Howard Street had a number of courts. There were courts and alleys attached to Denison Street. Cook's, Scales, Arthur's, Denison and Bell Court.

Kitty's health was still giving cause for alarm, which had not gone unnoticed by Mrs. Rathbone. Kitty was worried about the fate of her eldest son John Demontee. He had been at sea for some time, his ship was long overdue and the anxiety added to her poor state of health. She had after all every right to be alarmed, for the sea had claimed too many of Kitty's family. Mrs. Rathbone's intervention about Kitty's health sparked off a chain of events that was to give Kitty some reassurance about her son's welfare, She received a letter from Boston, written by Joseph Tuckerman on June the 10th, 1835:

My Dear Mrs. Wilkinson,

I have within a few days received a letter from our friend Mrs. Rathbone, who informs me that, at the date of her letter, you were indisposed, your health a good deal run down by cares and labours. I am concerned to learn this.

I do not mean that I feel any of that uneasiness which implies discontent with the government of our Heavenly Father. I am quite sure that he will do that only which is right and good with you with my self, aye with each of his children. This heavenly Father regards us, and every human being, with an infinitely greater love than that, which we have for our sons and daughters, and, if we believe in this love without a doubt, we shall trust in it, and in him, who feels it for us without reserve.

May the Heavenly Father help both you and me to understand and to feel the greatness of his love towards us, that so, we may love him more perfectly than we have ever yet loved him, and may resign ourselves at all times, and in every thing do his will! I have great pleasure in my recollection of the visit I made to you.

I shall never forget the hour I spent with you and your orphans. It was a holy hour. It was an hour to be remembered with joy in heaven. I have many delightful recollections of England, but I remember nothing there, which is more sacred in my thoughts and in my heart than the hour I spent in your little parlour.

But you have also been greatly blessed. God has crowned your life with the richest of the blessings with which he favours his children upon the earth. He has made you the honoured instrument of his own parental love to the poor children to whom you have been [as a mother.] You have thus been made a [worker together with God] for the salvation of his children. Oh! What, privilege, what honour, may be compared with this! And is your strength now failing?

Since you now give up your cares for those for whom you have so long cared, and toiled, and endured "Let not your heart be troubled; my dear friend, let it be the language of your heart—of your soul—behold God is my salvation, I will trust and not be afraid". You may indeed be called from that particular service for others, in which you have so long lived.

Yet that very service was but a school of preparation for a higher and nobler service for others, in the eternal life which is before you. I have no fear, than in dying we shall lose one of the principles or affections that have connected us with our God, with our Saviour, with our duties, and with the office of Christian love which may be performed towards any who may require them of us. The happiness of Heaven will be the happiness of [Christian Love] and, I believe also, of Christian Service.

Should this letter find you, as I think it may feeble and ill, may it find you also strong in the faith, the hopes, and the consolations of the Gospel you have, I am sure, wished to walk in. The steps of our great master, to live in this spirit of him who, "took little children into his arms, and blessed them" and "who went about doing good." May His Spirit within you now be the light, and strength, and joy of your soul.

I do not expect to see you again in this world. But I hope that I may be permitted to see you in the Everlasting Kingdom of our Father.

Mrs. Rathbone informs me that your son was sailing from Calcutta for Boston. We now have a sailor's reading room in this city, to which sailors resort while in port here. I have had a "notice" put up there in which I have requested that any seaman who shall know anything of John Demontee or John Wilkinson will bring me information concerning him. Ships often come here from Calcutta and if your son shall come to this city, I think that I shall hear of him. And if I can see him, you may be sure that he will find in me a friend. I shall be most grateful for any opportunity in any way of serving him.

Remember me to the children I saw with you, and tell them that it will rejoice my heart to hear that they are good children. I hope to hear of them through Mrs. Rathbone. Be assured that I am most truly your friend.

Joseph Tuckerman

Joseph Tuckerman, was born, in Boston, U S A. Jan. 18th 1778. He later studied for the "Unitarian Ministry" and he started The "Religious and Moral Improvement of Seamen" in 1812, an association which is said to have been the first of its kind in the United States.

His interest in seamen was duplicated by his interest in those he called "the neglected poor of our cities." He later began a "ministry-at-large," which was later to be known as a City Mission for the Poor. His book, "The Principles and Results of The Ministry at Large" which he wrote in Boston in 1838 describes his work and ideals.

In 1833-4 he established city missions for Seamen in London and Liverpool. On his return to Boston in 1836 his health broke down. In an attempt to improve his health in 1838 he went to Santa Cruz, he died two years later.

It is clear from the content of his letter that Kitty's health had broken down, and she was in a depressed state of mind. However it must have been a relief to her to know that her son was on his way to Boston. Kitty was as always strong in mind and she fought back, regaining the physical strength to look after her extended family.

The cholera was, for the moment, laid to rest and Kitty was still caring for other people, as well as the orphans that lived under her roof. The older children were finding employment working with families in the area. Joseph Tuckerman makes it clear from the tone of his letter a great friendship had developed between Kitty and Mrs. Rathbone. Kitty at this stage in her life would have been regarded as living to a great age; she was fifty years of old. Many people living in working class areas in the town would never reach forty years and even if they did they would be worn out.

For the next few years the town had plenty of work to offer the people, but by 1842 the nightmare of unemployment started all over again. This time it was not so much the fear of cholera but the dread of unemployment. Vauxhall Ward and was one of sixteen wards into which Liverpool was divided, and it had by this time stretched down river towards Bootle.

New places of employment gave more work to the towns-people - manufacturing was on the increase consisting of iron foundries, soap, alkali, chemical yards and other industries. They were supported by work within the area, the new emerging docks needing thousands of men to unload and load the ships, warehouses needed men to store the goods waiting for transit and the ships needed seamen.

So life in general was a little better despite bad housing and poor water supply. The council was at last tackling the question of supplying the working class with homes to rent. However those who controlled the town lost little sleep over the supply of water, they themselves had access to private wells and so water supply to them was not a problem.

The Vauxhall area, like the rest of the town, was still attracting more people to the new industries. The local business community of small traders felt more secure in opening shops to supply the needs of the community. More Courts, and Passages, containing tiny little houses were being built, still without a water supply.

After ten years, Kitty's efforts were at last recognised by the council when they decided to build a washhouse. A site was obtained in Upper Frederick Street and a building on a very humble scale was provided as an experiment. This was then the first public establishment of baths and washhouse in this country. They were opened on the 28th May 1842 and on the 11th October of the same year the Sub-Committee, to whom the management of the establishment was entrusted, made a report to the council.

Your Sub-Committee report that the baths and washhouse in Upper Frederick Street are now in full work. but your Sub-Committee regret that the ground on which they are erected is too confined for the purpose and too limited in space for the number who attend, and should the Corporation erect any other at the north end of the town, they recommend that the washhouses should be placed on the ground floor, (they were here in the basement). The drying room by hot-air pipes is far too small for the large quantity of clothes, from 300 to 400 dozen weekly, and in addition there should be a spacious yard to dry clothes with the sun and wind, which would be more healthy. In the erection of future baths your Sub-Committee recommend that the bathroom be placed so that there may be windows on both sides. That light and air be admitted, and made of such width that a division may be made down the middle that both sexes may bathe at any hour of the day.

This establishment at first contained a reading room but it was later converted into a bathroom.

By 1842, the progress that had been made in living conditions, and work, came to an end throughout Liverpool. The population of Vauxhall had risen from a few hundred people living mainly in the vicinity of Denison Street. to as many as 5,000 families, numbering about 24,000 individuals; and was about one-twelfth, of the population of Liverpool. Approximately one fifth of the ward's population, 1,000 families, were still resident in cellars where 1,236 families were lodgers without furniture. The latter consisted mainly of people who had pawned or sold all they possessed for food, and had taken to lodgings for shelter. It is easy to see why Kitty had taken so many lodgers into her home with all this misery around her.

Of 5,000 families, it was ascertained that,

1326	were natives of	Liverpool.
2243	" "	Ireland.
366	" "	Wales.
160	" "	Scotland.
106	" "	Isle of Man, and Foreigners.
776	" "	England generally.

With the exception of a small number of skilled tradesmen from Scotland, Lancashire, and Yorkshire, the rest were people newly arrived in the Vauxhall Ward from outlying agricultural districts.

Kitty Wilkinson

It was during this period that the North Corporation School, was established. This enabled some of the children to get a good plain education for the sum of one and a half pence per week. The School was conducted on similar principles to those adopted in the, Irish National Schools, and was very successful. The Irish National schools taught children of all denominations in the same school but they had separate religious instruction. However in Ireland it was also designed to bring about the demise of the Irish Language, only English was spoken in the schools. Many of the children in Liverpool during this period would be Welsh and Irish speakers.

However a resolution passed by the Liverpool Council, requiring from the pupils conformity to some of the usages of the Established Church resulted in the whole of the Catholic, and a portion of Protestant children, being withdrawn by their parents.

The proportion of children attending the school on average in October 1841, were 875 consisting of 386 boys, 284 girls, 205 infants. Four months later, under the new system in January 1842, attendance had dropped to 301 with 122 boys, 85 girls and 94 infants.

It was suggested that Kitty should play a part in setting up the "South Corporation School" and children of her own little school swelled the ranks of the new establishment. It is interesting to see how many parents of the children valued education when they were prepared to pay something towards their children's learning. At this time in 1842, Kitty was reaching the autumn of her life and she was still living in the same street in the Vauxhall Ward with Thomas.

John Finch, a local merchant and member of the Liverpool Anti-Monopoly Association, compiled a set of statistics paid for out of his own pocket to look into conditions of the poor in Vauxhall Ward. Some idea of the levels of poverty can be seen from letters sent to John Finch by local traders, for example Owen Williams a local House Agent wrote on 5th March, 1842.

I beg to return the manuscript copy of the tables, for the loan of which, please accept my thanks. I have long been aware that there was a great deal of wretchedness and destitution in Vauxhall Ward; but I was not aware it existed to so great an extent as you have exhibited. Before carefully examining the tables, I doubted their accuracy as to minutiae; but upon looking into the district books, from which they were compiled, and finding therein all my tenants names, occupations, &c, as correctly inserted as in my own "Collecting Books" I was convinced of their truth.

The description of their general condition I likewise find correct, with very few exceptions. The most cursory reader will perceive that you have bestowed much time, labour, and expense, in preparing the tables; but many of your readers will not credit their correctness, the wretchedness and destitution they depict being so heart rendering.

I assure you I find it very difficult to get in rents in Oriel, Banastre, and Blackstock Streets. The poor are so much reduced, that they are generally obliged to sub-let their houses to assist to pay the rent. Generally in such Streets. two families, and very often three (in each from two to five children), live in the same court house; but, notwith-standing this sub-letting, I am of the opinion that not more than three-fourths of the amount of rent is collected.

Frequently, also, the houses are unavoidably let under their value. All this mischief arises from want of employment. It is evident that monopoly will not furnish it, as we see this poverty and want of employment to co-exist with monopoly.

Talk about the agriculturists being subject to peculiar and heavy burdens; I doubt much if all the agriculturists' burdens were heaped upon one of our rich land-lords, he would feel as intensely as one of the poor hungry, starving, fellows of Vauxhall Ward. I have long been of the opinion that hundreds die in this town from gradual starvation.

Owen Williams, was one of many business and trades people who wrote to John Finch and Liverpool Anti-Monopoly Association. The following are a sample of letters he received from other traders, and shopkeepers in the Vauxhall Ward. You will see by the following letters how most people in the community suffered, none more so than the working class. However it also shows how many businesses were ruined, and yet those same traders still had time to think about those less fortunate than themselves.

18th February, 1842.

I have been in business twenty-five years as a flour dealer and bread baker, wholesale and retail, and my business is principally with the working class. When provisions are dear, the working classes are not only compelled to buy less quantities, but the worst quantities. As regards the extent of my business at the present time, I am not doing more than three-fifths of what I was doing in 1835 and 1836. You must likewise understand that flour and bread, in those years, was only half as much for the money as it is now.

It was of a much superior quality; for instance, flour was then ten and twelve pounds for the shilling. Whilst, at the present time, it is only five to six pounds; and, in those years, there was plenty of work, and every article proportionally cheap; and at the same time, higher wages.

The contrast of the working classes at that period and now must be sufficiently clear.

The demand for labour has been gradually declining for several years, and the rate of wages, to my certain knowledge, has been declining also for the same period. At the same time provisions have been getting dearer; therefore, it is evident that the labouring class have been growing worse in their circumstances for the same number of years. Till at last they are reduced to a condition considerably worse than paupers in the workhouse in fact, they are starving with hunger.

As regards the flour trade, in which I am engaged, when compared with 1835, it must be infinitely worse for me, as a greater capital is required. This in consequence of wheat being dearer, and less consumption and less profits, owing to the working class being unemployed. The depression in trade is felt now most seriously, and I attribute it entirely to the want of employment, and the restrictions that are employed by our corn laws and commercial code.

Edward Weston Naylor St.

18th February, 1842.

I have been in business as a flour dealer and bread baker, thirty-three years, in Liverpool, and all that time in Vauxhall Road. My trade is principally the working class, and I find when provisions, &c., are dear (and this is my experience) that Labour is scarce the working classes purchase not only less quantities, but the worst qualities; and this I am sure is always the case.

I am not doing so much business, when compared with former years say, five or six years ago by one half. I certainly never knew so much distress among the working class as there is at the present: we have nearly as many beggars as customers. I consider the corn laws, and other restrictions, are the principal causes of our embarrassment.

Richard Haskayne. Vauxhall Rd.

11th, February 1842.

I have resided in Liverpool twenty-six years, and for fifteen of that time have kept a shop for the sale of provisions, principally to the working classes. I find that my sales during the last year, as compared with 1835, have fully diminished, one-half, and the food they purchase is of the worst kind, now, as compared with the former year.

From my own knowledge, the condition of the working classes has been getting worse and worse for several years past. I have sustained great losses within the last few years. I attribute the present bad trade mainly to the obnoxious corn laws, and, in a great degree, to the other restrictions on commerce which prevent the poor man his fair share of employment.

Patrick M'Sheane

12th February, 1842.

I have resided in Liverpool nearly fourteen years, and am by trade a shoemaker; when I came to Liverpool, I found work very easy to be obtained. I afterwards commenced business on my own account, eight years ago; up to 1835, my business was steadily on the increase. Since that time, notwithstanding greater exertions on my part, a more extensive stock, a greater number of my friends, and less competition, in the immediate neighbourhood, my business has been greatly on the decline, more particularly during the last two years: the present time is worst of all.

Nearly the whole of my business is amongst the working classes; and, owing to the high price of provisions, and scarcity of employment, a greater portion of children, of both sexes, are compelled to go bare-footed, up to fourteen or fifteen years of age. And many others, of all ages, are under the necessity of wearing such articles as they themselves would not pick up on the Street, were they in constant employment, at moderate wages.

I know from past experience, that my weekly receipts would be more, by six or seven pounds, were trade moderately good. At the present time, articles of the most inferior description are most in request. The condition of the working classes has been getting worse since 1837, but far more rapidly during the last twelve months. People are less able to pay shoe bills at present than during any time since I have been in business; and I am afraid I have made more bad debts during the two years, than during the other six.

The present distress is owing to the working classes being unable to obtain employment, and that would no doubt be removed by a repeal of the corn laws, which would make provisions cheaper, and work more plentiful, for we could then exchange our goods for foreign corn. Several instances have occurred to me, during the last two years, of men that I have been obliged to discharge for want of work, offering to work for less wages, if I could give them constant employment. It is scarcity of work, and not cheap bread that reduces wages.

Wm. Machan. 136, Vauxhall Rd.

The following letter is from one of the parties engaged in collecting statistics for the Liverpool Anti-Monopoly Association.

I have been employed to collect information in Scotland Road, Mary-bone, Vauxhall Road, Great Howard Street, and Waterloo Road, concerning the condition of the people in those neighbourhoods. Many of the shopkeepers informed me, that they had not taken sufficient ready-money of late to pay their rent and taxes. One shopkeeper stated, he only took eight shillings, during the previous week; and on the day I called, from morning until one o'clock, he had received only one penny. several shopkeepers stated that they were under the necessity of pledging various articles to pay their rent and taxes.

I found, also, the pawnbrokers heavily complaining of being almost at a standstill for want of money, from the great quantity of articles pledged, and their customers being unable to redeem them, as weekly customers used to do. The general complaint is the depression in trade, and want of employment, which is every day getting worse.

The high prices of all kinds of provisions, at the present time, without any advance of wages to the few that are employed, is considered to be a great hardship, and a principal cause of the present distress.

They all well remember six years ago, when potatoes were 4 pence, per peck; flour from 9 lbs, to 12 lbs, for a l shilling; butcher's meat equally low, and bacon little more than half the present price.

Few labouring people know the taste of fresh meat; and numbers of respectable-looking persons, without any solicitation, express, with their own free-will, that, in numbers of instances, they partake of only two meals a-day, while the working-people, very frequently, can only obtain one scanty meal, scarcely sufficient to support nature. Many persons that I have visited consider that, if the corn laws were repealed, employment would be increased.

Many of the lodgers, in this district, are out of employment, and supported by the people they lodge with, but their lodging-house-keepers, being mostly poor, will be under the necessity of turning them into the Street, if something is not done to give them employment or relief."

Thos Sammond.
Liverpool, January 1842

Again we have an extract from a letter written by John Holme. Engaged by the Anti-Monopoly Association to ascertain the conditions of the inhabitants of the Vauxhall Ward.

A family, with five children, had not an article of furniture, except an old chair and table. With apparently a few old rags in one corner of the room for a bed, with a horse-cloth for a covering for the whole seven.

But it is unnecessary to mention solitary cases. I could name some hundreds that are in the same condition, some having neither food nor fire, and living on one, or it may be

two, meals a day; in most instances, only potatoes and salt.
And some even with nothing more than a Swedish turnip
boiled, in the course of the day, for a family of six. Indeed,
there are whole Courts in the greatest possible state of
destitution. In one Street I found a Court of only six houses,
containing no less then sixty-seven individuals, in the
greatest distress, all their houses being so miserably
furnished that I would not have had all they contained as a
gift.

The reason there are so many persons huddled together is,
they cannot pay their rents without taking lodgers. The rent,
in most instances, they are obliged to pay, even if they go
without food, although I found, in some instances, that the
landlords were willing to wait until things were better.

Another extract from a similar letter to the Anti-monopoly
Association highlights the importance of the roll of local
charitable institutions.

Many would be found dead in their houses but for the
exertions of the District Provident Society, and other
charitable institutions, backed by private charity.

The residences of some of the people, particularly in
Harrison Street, are beyond description; lying on cold damp
floors, with but a couple of inches of straw, which, from the
nature of the ground, must be soon soaked through.

This final letter to the Anti-monopoly Association, came from
Edward Partridge, a shop keeper in Denison Street. Kitty must
have known Edward Partridge, and possibly lived only a few
doors from his shop.

I have been fourteen years in the bread and provision trade,
and my business is principally with the working classes. I

am sure that they were never in such great distress as they are at the present time; they not only purchase a considerably less quantity, but the most inferior description of provisions; and want of employment is daily making their conditions worse.

I am not doing as much business by one-third as I was in former years. I consider the want of employment amongst the labouring classes, and the heavy restrictions that are placed on our commerce, are the causes of the existing distress. Monopolies of every description I consider an evil."

Edward Partridge, Denison St.

What those letters show is a genuine concern by many of the trades people in the town for the plight of the poor. Kitty's efforts had not gone unnoticed. Her work was still being carried forward by good Christian people, such as William and Margaret Rathbone. The local charity's organised by the ladies of the town saved many from starving to death by raising money to help the poor. They were the people who would influence others to fight for better conditions for the people of the town.

Although ten years had elapsed since the first outbreak of cholera, living conditions for most of Kitty Wilkinson's neighbours had changed very little. It is not surprising Kitty's health suffered during this period. Like most people in Liverpool and elsewhere she would be lucky to have a doctor to turn to for help. Liverpool, like most towns, had very few physicians, and they were there to serve only those who could afford their services. As late as 1829 just a few years before the first signs of cholera, Liverpool had only twenty-nine physicians and they all lived at the top end of the town, and none near the tens of thousands in the lower part of the town.

Wherever the newly arrived poor settled in the town the unscrupulous builders and landlords built hovels, thus helping to cause a sea of misery for those who had to find shelter in them. Vauxhall Ward had more than its fair share of them, contained in the following list are just some of the Courts.

List of Streets, Courts, etc. in Vauxhall Ward

List of Streets, Courts, etc. in Vauxhall Ward
Divided into 38 Districts

St. = Street.   Ct. = Court.   Pl. = Place.
Bldgs. = Buildings.   Sq. = Square.   Rd. = Road:

No. 1   Edgar St. Edgar Ct.

No 2   Parker Ct.

No 3   Cavendish St. Weston Ct. Howe's Ct. Tamer's Pl. Knowle's Pl. Evan's Ct. Clayton Ct. Atherton Ct. M'Curdy's Ct. Schofield Ct.

No 4   Milton St. Kilshaw Ct. James Ct. Tarbock Sq. Bloomsbury Bldgs. Kilshaw Pl. Allison's Pl. Humphrey's Ct. Thomas Bldgs. Henshaw Pll. Rigby Pl. Peyton Pl. Willow Pl. Charter Pl. John Sq. Union Pl.

No 5   Harrison St. Hughes Ct. Leech Ct.

No 6   Sawney Pope St Cecilia Pl. Jones Ct. Britannia Pl. Mercer. Emmett Pl.

No 7   Addison St John's Ct. Madder Pl. Barton's Ct. Addison Ct. Priscilia Pl.

No 8   Vine Pl. Chisenhale Ct. Skelhorne Ct. Prescott Ct. Cottage Pl. Priscila Pl.

No 9   Chadwick St. Mariners Ct.

No 10   Wigan St. Night Ct.

No 11   Charters St. Williams Ct. Fir Ct. Summer Ct. Restriction
Pl. Deal Pl.   Ash Ct. Oak Pl. Catherine Ct. Mathew Ct.
Whitton Ct. Threlfall Ct.   Elizabeth Pl. Woodward
Bldgs. Charter Pl.

No 12   Eaton St. M oss Ct. Pierce Ct. Carson Ct. Calvert   C t .
Rose Ct.   Keally's Ct. Robert's Ct. Mason Ct. Pye
Ct. Ford Bldgs.

No 13   Gascoyne St. Hunter's Pl. Gascoyne Ct. Abram Ct. Nile
Ct.   Baylies Ct. Glouscester Ct. Nelson Ct. Sutton Ct.
St. Vincent Ct. Goodman Ct. John Ct.

No 14   Mahon St. Emma Ann St. Ellam's Ct. Agnes Ct.
Parkinson Pl.

No 15..

No 16   Paul St. Davies Pl. Ann's Pl. Paul Pl. Donkin's Ct.
Donkin's Bldgs. Felicity Pl. Harriett Pl. May's Pl. Castle
Pl. Roland Pl. William's Pl. Jones Pl. Elias Pl.

No17   Cherry Ln.

No 18   Oriel St. Daly's Pl. and Ct. Glob Bldgs. Nancy's Ct.
John's Ct.   Webster's Ct. Webster's Bldgs. Carson Ct.
Elizabeth Ct. Jones Ct. Robinson Pl. Hilton's Ct.
Thomson's Ct. Pinnington Ct. OxfordCt. Halsall's Bldgs.
Clough's Bldgs. Huge's Pl. Oriel Pl.   Bridget Pl.
Rodick Pl. Holland Ct.

No 19   Naylor St. Harmony Pl. Mathew's Pl. Mary's Bldgs. Queen's Ct. Moss Ct. Ward's Ct. Moss Bldgs. Parr's Ct. Wellington Ct. Naylor Pl. Morrall   Ct. Mill Ct. Nailor Ct.

No 20   Freemason's Row. Garden Pl. Barrow Ct. Houlding's Ct. Davies Ct. Goslin Ct. Chandler Ct. Darwin Ct.

No 21   Gladstone St. Crennill's Pl. Edward's Pl. Thomas Pl. George's Pl. Standish Ct. Old Dock Ct. Becket's Pl. Emigration Pl. Taylor's   Bldgs. St. George's Pl. Reform Ct. Mary's Ct. Munro's Bldgs.

No 22   Robert St. North. Greenock St. Paisley St. Albion Place Galton St.   Barton St. North. Dundee St. Neptune St. Crompton St. Oil St.

No 23   Denison St. Cook's Ct. Scales Ct. Arthur's Ct. Denison Ct. Bell Ct.

No 24   Stewart St. Wilson's Pl. Rebecca Pl. Wood's Pl. Naylor's Pl. William's Pl. Edward's Pl. Adam Pl. Betsy Pl. Eliza Pl. Bridget Pl. Margaret Pl. James Pl. Salop Pl. Clontare Pl. Friendship Pl. Pritchard Pl. Robert Pl.   Daniel Pl. Jane Pl. Priscilla Pl. Mary's Pl. Kirkman's Pl. Frederick's Pl. John's Pl. Neston Pl. Moreland Pl. Douglas Pl. Top Pl.

No 25   Leeds St. Summer Ct. Wilkinson Ct. Troughear's Ct. Pilkington Ct. Roberts Ct. Carpenter's Ct. Plumber St. Holland Ct. Rockcliffe Ct.

No 26   Carruthers St. Carruthers Ct. Hargreaves Ct. Evans Pl.

No 27   Banastre St. Ellen's Ct. Mary's Ct. Mainwareham Ct.

Kilshaw Ct. Thomas Ct. Lewis Bldgs. Spring Ct. Union Ct. Jones Ct.

No 28 Arley St. Summer Pl. Williams Ct. Forbiss Bldgs. Jones Pl. Middlem Pl. Rogerson's Pl. Hughes Pl. Hughes Ct. Prim Pl. Newal's Bldgs. Summer Seat Marshall Pl. Carter's Ct.

No 29 Gildart's Gardens. Bush Pl. Carpenter's Sq. Davies Ct. Mary's Pl. Mason's Ct. No. 57. Ct. Pratchet Ct. Parker's Ct. St. George's Pl. Trotter's Ct. Tyrer's Ct. Wilson's Ct.

No 30 Maguire St. Ellenthorpe Ct. Burn's Pl. Davies Ct. Hodgson Ct. Ebenezer Pl. Liver Passage.

No 60 Court. John's Ct. Wyatt Ct. Chapel Ct. Hindle Ct. Warren's Ct. Elizabeth Pl. Taylor's Pl. Rhode Pl. Didsbury Pl. Stopperth Pl. Rowland's Pl. Dillon's Bldgs. Pl. Emigration Pl. Taylor's Bldgs. St. George's Pl. Reform Ct. Mary's Ct. Munro's Bldgs.

No 32 Blackstock St. Battersby's Pl. Canning Pl. Maind Pl. Providence Pl. Economy Pl. Mary's Pl. Margaret's Ct. Margaret's Pl. No. 59. Ct.

No 53 Scotland Rd. Back Milton St. Bevington Bush. Marybone. Bevington Bush Rd. Gardiner's Row. Limekiln Ln. Summer Pl. Albert Pl. Marybone Pl. Parker Ct.

No 34 Vauxhall Rd. Parter's Ct. Elizabeth Ct. Weston Ct.

No 35 Great Howard St. Waterloo Rd. Rotunda Pl. Gibraltar St. Gibraltar Pl. Canal Ct.

No 36   Fontenoy St.

No 37   Stockdale St. Rowlin's Pl. William's Pl. Hope Pl. Allen's
Ct. William's Ct. Bain's Ct.

No 38   Midghall Ln. Bell's Pl. William's Ct. Joiner's Pl.
Harmony Pl. Ford's   Ct. Midghall St.

8

Kitty and Queen Victoria

The name of Kitty Wilkinson and her work for the poor of the town had not gone unnoticed by the town council and leading members of the community. In 1846 Liverpool decided it would honour Kitty for all her great work. She and her husband Thomas were invited to Carnatic Hall, Woolton, which at that time was outside the Liverpool boundary. Kitty had been told that she was to meet Queen Victoria, and other members of the Royal Family. She had no idea her achievement in combatting cholera and work for the poor had come to the notice of the Queen. Also present at Carnatic Hall were Mrs George Lawrence, the Mayoress of Liverpool. Queen Victoria presented Kitty with a silver tea-service which included a teapot engraved with the words.

"The Queen the Queen Dowager and the ladies of Liverpool to Catherine Wilkinson 1846.'

Kitty was 60 years of age at this time and still had a lot of energy left in her. This was also the time she and Thomas were offered the position of Superintendents of the new washhouse at 135 Upper Frederick Street. Taking up this appointment could not have been easy for Kitty, as it meant leaving Denison Street where she had spent most of her life. Denison Street had been the spring board for most of her work, the street where the world's first public washhouse came into being. The post of Superintendent of the new washhouse came about through the intervention of William Rathbone

An article in the *Daily Post & Mercury*. Tuesday, January 6, 1925. Reported:

> *Posted recently in Great Britain an envelope bearing the motto, "Commune Bonum." of the Hong Kong Club, and addressed:*
>
>> *The Chairman*
>>
>> *Health Committee,*
>>
>> *Town Hall, Liverpool*
>
> *has been handed to Alderman Muirhead. Enclosed was a lithographed copy with footnote of a letter inserted in the "Economist," on or about 1846, and reproduced by a lithographic writer for the convenience of the author (William Rathbone) in answering correspondents.*
>
> *The copy is dated "Liverpool, 26th January 1848," and signed "W. Rathbone" both date and signature apparently written by the same hand."*
>
> *The authenticated circular contains some 1,200 words telling the Kitty Wilkinson story. It would certainly exert a wide influence by assisting in the extension of public washhouses to allow the efficient dealing with clothes and bedding during periods when disease was rampant. The Daily Post and Mercury also featured a report by William Rathbone to gain further support for the building of washhouses.*
>
> *P.S. This letter, originally inserted in the 'Economist' in*

answer to some questions in that paper has been asked for in cases where funds for larger establishments could not be raised. I shall be glad to give any further information in my power as to the washing of this humble wash-house, which may be desired by any persons wishing to commence a similar one.

The only addition which now occurs to me is to press strongly the importance, [particularly to the sick] of sufficient means of drying the clothes thoroughly and quickly.

When we consider the smallness of the fires of the poor, and their want of change of clothes, we see in most cases the almost inevitable consequence must be using them damp, with all the train of illness attendant upon such a practice.

The two Liverpool establishments and those in London, which I have seen, excellent as they are, are greatly defective in this particular.

William Rathbone gave a clear picture of the first wash-house, basic as it was, when started by Kitty Wilkinson and the upgrading of the wash-house, when the District Provident Society lent their aid. Even as early has 1837 other towns and cities had seen what had taken place in Liverpool, and had taken the first steps in improving conditions in their own towns. William Rathbone brought, not just to the notice of the Liverpool council, but the whole nation, the great need for further improvements in wash-house facilities to ease the suffering of ordinary people. William Rathbone continued to write to the council in support of Kitty and Thomas. The District Provident Society also supported Kitty's application, as shown in their letters to the council.

Kitty Wilkinson

Gentlemen

The singularity of the case must be my excuse for bringing the application of Mr. and Mrs. Wilkinson for the situation of Superintendents of the Baths and Washhouses in Frederick Street, before the members of the town council in this common manner, instead of confining myself to giving my testimony in their favour in the committee, with whom the recommendation to your appointment naturally rests.

I would request your attention to the subjoined extract from the correct account of. "The Origin of the Liverpool Baths and Wash-houses," Published in the Historical Register, Jan 1845; and I would appeal to you, whether the Institution itself, owing its origin to her benevolent and self-denying activity, and its prosperity, and the subsequent adoption by the Corporation. To her clever management, does not give her a claim above other applicants, if she and her husband are found fully competent to carry it on.

Her talents for management and for economy may be judged by the fact, that, in one week of August, 1833, she washed, dried, and returned to their rightful owners.

34 beds,
158 sheets,
110 blankets,
60 quilts,
140 dozen of clothes,

All infected with cholera, at an expense of less than £6. 120 of these sheets were lent.

Her health is now much better, and her strength greater, than at any former period in her life; and her experience, with the absence of young children, [not having young children to look after] I consider her as far more than counterbalancing her age, which is, I believe, about 56. Her husband is some years younger than herself, and as his wife seemed the natural person to be appointed to the management of the Baths, and the young man who put up the machinery lodged with them at the time, he [Thomas] watched its erection, until he considered himself fully acquainted with his part of the duties which might be required.

I am anxious about the appointment of Mr. and Mrs. Wilkinson, believing that their active benevolence, and fearlessness of infection, are very uncommon, and it is only by such that the washing of infested clothes will be carried out to its full capability.

I am anxious about it for its effect upon the poor, as encouragement to follow her example. No danger of fatigue has deterred her from sitting up with the sick; and she and her husband have worked hard, and lived hard, to support orphans whose only claim upon them was the remembrance of the kindness they had received when left orphans themselves. Many of the children had claims on the parish, but these were never urged; and 2s a week which one child was receiving at the time they took charge of him, and 5s, which five others were receiving, was at once returned; and a remission of her payment of her poor rates is all she has ever received for her care. The South Corporation Infant School arose from a number of children she had collected in her bed-room whose parents were ill of cholera.

Their means of supplying this extensive benevolence were their own hard earnings, he as a labourer, until lately, when he has kept a coal cellar, and she has cleaned offices and kept lodgers, often those who were sick and unable to pay.

I need not, I am sure, after this statement, press upon your attention the importance of showing our estimation of such conduct, by letting Mrs. Wilkinson reap its natural reward in the management of the institution which owes its beginning to her, and for which she has proved herself so well qualified nor the discouragement which its refusal will be to such independence, and fearless self denying benevolence.

Yours respectfully

William Rathbone

The following letter also refers to Kitty, after the Provident District Society discontinued their help due to lack of funds. She continued with her little wash-house, despite the fact that Kitty had to use every penny her husband earned, to continue to help the poor:-

Mr. Campbell and Mr. Lawerence, and the members of the committee of the Provident District Society, from 1832 to 1837, when the low state of the funds obliged them to discontinue their assistance to the washing cellar, can bear testimony to the truth of this statement, as can any of the medical men appointed to that district of the town. There are in the Town-Hall strong testimonials from some of them, and from Mr. Alan Hodgson, who has known her most of her life, and numerous others."

By 1836 The Unitarians had founded a domestic mission and placed the Rev. John Johns in charge. Like Kitty Wilkinson he worked amongst the poor in trying to improve living conditions. Kitty's work must have been known to Rev. John Johns, who was the first minister of the Domestic Mission in Liverpool in 1836, just four years after the first out-break of cholera in the town.

The son of an artist who painted in the style of Turner, the Rev. Johns born in Northhill Plymouth liked to write poetry, and he composed a number of hymns, some of which were published.

The committee which chose Rev. Johns, set him to work as its minister in St. James Street, Greenland Street and Upper Frederick Street. As soon as Johns brought his family to Liverpool, he asked the Rev. Thom to show him the district. Thom said.

He remembered how, as he walked through the streets in silence with the Rev Johns searching out its worst places, gazing into cellars and up into lighted rooms, pausing before the many premises in which alcoholic spirits were sold, that he could feel that solemn purposes were forming in Johns' heart.

The Rev. Thom was the minister of the church were Kitty and Thomas worshipped. In Johns' first report, dated September, 1837, five years after the start of the cholera, he declared:

During these months I have seen things that had surpassed my imagination I have seen life under forms, which took from it, all that in my eyes, made it happy, hopeful, or even human.

The Rev. Johns could only believe the sufferings of the poor were unknown to the rich, otherwise, long before this they would have done something to alleviate conditions. His first winter among the crowded alleys was a winter of unemployment. He had attempted as best he might to give relief, but all he had at his disposal amounted to £24 and he fully realised administering relief was not enough. At this time, because of an expanding Empire, England was a rich and powerful country in the world. In stark contrast death from starvation was a frequent occurrence amongst its inhabitants.

The Rev. Johns recognised the difficulties of the poor regarding education, which was scarcely within reach. Reading, writing, sewing, and common rules of arithmetic were all that could ever be learned if a child was lucky enough to be able to attend a school. After just seven months in the post as minister, Johns wished to see experiments in free education, he also wanted to encourage a taste for reading.

He saw so much misery, hopelessness and drunkenness, he believed that people were drawn into Liverpool in the hope of improving their position in the world. Indeed he believed they might do so, if it were not for the temptations which were always at hand, from ale-houses and spirit-shops when he wrote:

> *A man cannot go to his work or return from it, without passing; perhaps, a dozen of those fearful places, in which he is tempted, at first to forget the duties of life, and afterwards to renounce and despise them. None who have looked into the state of the Liverpool poor, can fail to be struck with the amount of negative and positive religion among them. The Catholic priests were too few in number to do more than go when summoned, and therefore urged the establishment of a Roman Catholic ministry to the poor. The poor live and die in a Christian land; but neither their lives nor their welfare have anything to do with Christianity.*

In the first report by Johns it was felt that it ended on a note of hope. Soon, he believed, with the help of friends, whose names he would not mention, as he knew them to be those who do good by stealth, and would blush to find their names announced. *"Do what you will with humanity, you cannot wholly quench the divine ray within it."* What Johns and his friends hoped to achieve we can never be sure, but who were those friends? It may well have been William Rathbone and other people of influence in the town.

The Rev. Johns also regarded living conditions of the poor as an evil, and a leading cause of their distress:

> *Streets for the most part dark and narrow, dirty and ill*

paved; houses which are very often in the worst possible repair, rooms in lodging houses which are deficient in every important requisite conducive to health, convenience, and decency; garrets through which the winter wind often finds its way to many a shiver's bosom; cellars which, though in some instances, they are dry and commodious, yet are more usually damp, dark, and ruinous, and more like graves dug for the living than their homes. These regions of dreariness and darkness are closely beset with courts, in some of which it would be a still greater penalty to live, than in the streets from which they diverge.

Johns, like Kitty, was a visionary, a man who was not prepared to accept that nothing could be done for those living without hope, in the most degrading conditions. He proposed that people should have the right to free schooling, visiting committees for supervising the sending of children to school. Reduced terms for suitable youths at some of the higher schools of the town and opening of museums and other institutions to the poor on certain days.

He also called for payment of wages on Fridays instead of Saturdays and employers taking an interest in the welfare of employees. More visits for purely benevolent as opposed to proselytising purposes by the clergymen of all denominations. Public readings and free lectures to remove the very real abuse of making wage-payments late on Saturday nights. This was the world of Kitty Wilkinson, who did not divorce herself from it. She was able to breathe and smell this poverty twenty four hours every day of her life and it moulded her thinking and the toughness of her character. She became one of the corner stones of the town of Liverpool because she believed it was people that mattered and she had seen people being treated in the most vile way most of her life.

John Finch, a witness before the Commons Committee on

Intoxication among the labouring classes in 1834, had described the method of paying dock labourers in Liverpool, whose wages varied between one and three shillings a day. The Dockers were engaged by about a hundred and twenty men called "lumpers," who contracted with the merchants for loading and discharging the vessels, he wrote:

> *That there were not more than one or two out of the 120 that paid their workmen anywhere else than at a public house; some of them kept public houses themselves; and it was, and still is, the practice to meet the workmen at public houses early on Saturday evening and to keep out of the way till 10, 11, 12, then the shops would be closed before they could go to purchase the articles wanted for their families. In many cases half their wages were expended in the public houses before they received the rest.*

The Rev. Johns, became involved with the poor in so many diverse ways, he called for, and got, the use of 16 acres of land to let it as allotments for all by local people.

The land continued to be used until Lord Sefton, took it back to build houses. Those houses today, stand on each side of Prince's Road. Johns also called for open spaces and a convalescent home on the Wirral, at Egremont or New Brighton. He campaigned for more understanding and respect for each other regardless of denomination.

A description of the town comes over as the visionary and romantic poet that Johns was:

> *A large, distinguished and city-like town, seated like a new Tyre or Venice by the tributary waters, a mart of commerce, a theatre for splendour, a nursery for art, for energy, and for refinement.*

The Rev. Johns in a letter to the Albion newspaper supported a demand for a reduction of hours, in the working week for Governesses and Dressmakers. By 1846 victims of the famine in Ireland started to arrive in great numbers and Rev. Johns showed great concern for their welfare. Many showed the marked effects of starvation or were already gripped by signs of the fever, but very little help was at hand.

In 1847 300,000 people arrived in Liverpool having escaped the famine in Ireland and about 80,000 stayed on in the town, many finishing up in the fever sheds at Brownlow Hill. Rev. John Johns in his annual report revealed the awful plight of the poor:

Mothers, newly become such, without a garment on their persons, and infants nearly as naked, lying upon straw or shavings, under a miserable covering, without fire or food, or the means of procuring them; children taken from their schools, in order to earn by begging........infirm or aged people, who were shivering out their last hours of life in absolute want.

On the 23rd of June, 1847, the Rev. Johns died from contracting cholera in the course of removing the body of a victim from a cellar. With the exception of a Catholic priest, no other person would touch the body, it was said:

He died in the execution of his duty, a martyr to the cause of social and religious progress.

We may never be sure what part Kitty played in easing the suffering, of victims of the famine. We know by now she was turned sixty and had taken on the responsibility of superintendent with her husband Thomas of the new wash-house. However it is almost certain that she did play a part in caring for famine victims.

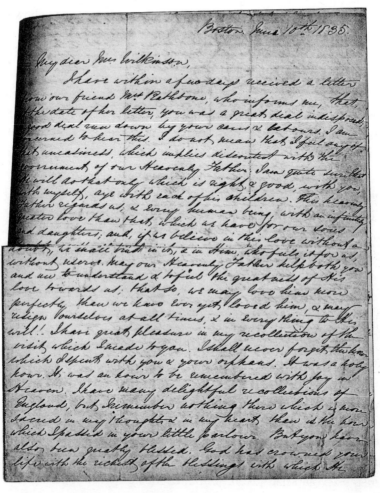

Extract. Letter from Joseph Tuckerman to Kitty, June 10, 1835

9

William Rathbone

The Rathbone family origins can be traced to Gawsworth, near Macclesfield where the first William Rathbone was born in 1669. Hisson, William II, born on 22 May 1698, left Gawsworth for the growing port of Liverpool where he worked as a sawyer and later established a timber business. William Rathbone II was the first member of the family to join the Society of Friends, or 'Quakers', in 1726. His son William III also became a member and he in turn passed his teachings on to his son William Rathbone IV.

William found it difficult to accept its doctrines in the same way that his father and grandfather had in the early 19th century. However, the Quaker characteristics of industry and zeal to right social wrongs were to pervade in later generations. The family business expanded during the 19th century and established an international merchant concern. This in turn led to a series of partnerships and creation of Rathbone Brothers & Co. in 1824.

The birth place of William Rathbone V, was Liver Street, off Park Lane, Liverpool in 1787. It was at that time a very fashionable quarter of the town. The 'Liverpool Mercury' commenting on the area of 1787 wrote:

There were no docks to shut out a view of the river; and anywhere beyond Hanover Street in that direction, so comparatively limited in size was Liverpool then, was considered almost in the suburbs.

A year later in 1788 his father William Rathbone IV leased a residence near Liverpool to house his family in a country environment which he then purchased in 1809. The name of the property was Greenbank, and remained the family home for over a century. William Rathbone was from a family whose name has been honourably associated with the city ever since Liverpool became commercially important. The family also had a house at Cornhill, the site of the present Albert dock. It was then the custom of merchants to live near their place of business and to superintend, in a more personal manner. Even after succeeding his father in business he continued to reside at "the counting-house" in Cornhill, while his widowed mother occupied Greenbank.

In 1812 he married Elizabeth Greg, daughter of Samual Greg of Quarry Bank, Manchester. They had five children. As the Gregs were Unitarians, William Rathbone had, according to the discipline of the Society of Friends, incurred the penalty of expulsion by marrying out of the body. He was later readmitted upon his giving an assurance that, though he could not out of courtesy to his wife say he repented having married her, he would not do it again.

Some years later he and his family finally severed their connection with the Society and joined a congregation of Unitarians. At the time of his marriage, William Rathbone was deeply immersed in politics, helping to organise various petitions in favour of reform. That period in the early part of the 19th Century was one of great poverty and suffering and consequent discontent. However the Government blamed "political agitators" who were working for reform. Strong measures were taken to suppress the evil. The Habeas Corpus Act was suspended and the right to hold public meetings taken away.

Lists of suspected persons especially members of the Reform Party, all over the country were prepared and their movements spied on. William Rathbone's name was seen by a friend of the Rathbone family, in one of the lists. Those lists were prepared for Lord Castlereagh.

In 1835 William Rathbone was elected a Liberal councillor for Liverpool and offered the Mayoralty but declined it at that time. In 1837, Mr. Rathbone was elected Mayor of Liverpool and in proposing him Mr. W. Wallace Currie said:

> *The gentleman whom I am about to propose has always held a more prominent position in the public eye than any individual in Liverpool and has received on the one hand more warm applause from those who admire him and approve his political principles and on the other more censure from those who disapprove of them.*
>
> *In the whole course of his public career, he has steered a straightforward course, unmindful of censure or praise, consulting only that which he believed to be for the public good, and persevering through evil report and good report until he has at last obtained the proud-eminence of being respected by those who do not approve of his conduct, and admired and beloved by those that do.*

As Mayor he laid the foundation stone of St. George's Hall. He took a strong stand against bribery and other forms of corruption existing in municipal elections and was an active supporter of the Municipal Reform Act of 1835. The Corporation owned two elementary schools, supported out of the rates and maintained 'on the principles of the Church of England.' This arrangement had always seemed to the Reformers unjust to all dissenting sects, but more especially to Roman Catholics, who formed the majority of the poorest section of the community.

As soon as Mr. Rathbone's party found themselves in a majority on the council, a committee decided to introduce what was known as the Irish National school system. The children all received secular instruction together and then Protestants and Catholics were separated to receive religious instruction. This arrangement was accepted by the Catholics but Rev. Hugh M'Neil was very much against it. He saw this as a way of dealing a blow at the Catholics and undermining the Liberal Party in the council.

From the pulpit and meetings, together with sections of the press, a campaign was waged against Corporation schools which lasted for four years. A cry of 'No Popery' stimulated the actions of those opposed to Corporation schools until they got their way. The Whigs steadily lost ground, until, in 1841, thirteen Tory candidates were elected out of sixteen. William Rathbone who sat for Pit Street Ward, was one of those who lost. He soon returned to the council as member for Vauxhall Ward, but in 1850 was again thrown out, this time on the question of the water supply. He had been chairman of the committee that carried the Rivington Pike scheme, which was denounced by people outside of the Council as unnecessarily extensive and extravagant.

After the defeat of the Whigs on the educational question, William Rathbone and his wife turned their attention to the Hibernian Schools and succeeded in making them, for their day, model elementary schools. The religious instruction was managed upon the Irish system where Catholic and Protestant sat together side by side. The schools became noted for the number and excellence of the teachers whom they trained. William Rathbone outlived the scorn poured on him by those opposed to his political and theological views.

He was remembered for his zeal in every cause of social and civic improvement and benevolence to the poor. At the time of his unpopularity the council declined to have his portrait hung in the council chamber. It was later unearthed from obscurity in the Mechanics Institute and hung in the Council Chamber. The Rathbones always made their home a kind of general rendezvous for all visitors to Liverpool who had some special opinion to propagate, or some philanthropic scheme to advance.

Many of the people who stayed at Greenbank, home of the Rathbones, are household names today. They included, John James Audubon, (c.1780-1851) the American naturist borne in Louisiana. He was known for his study of mammals in America and bird drawings. Robert Owen, (1771-1858) born Newton Montgomeryshire Scotland, socialist founder of New Lanark and New Harmony. Owen's main principle was that the best work can only be expected from happy prosperous and educated people. Blanko White, former Spanish priest, (1775-1841) born at Seville of an Irish family. He gave up the priesthood to embrace Unitarianism. He was also an author, his works include Letters from Spain, 1822. Rathbone's guests also included Lady Byron and William Roscoe. Another was Fr. Theobold Mathew, the temperance reformer, (1790-1856) well known in Cork, Ireland for his work among the poor. Mathew was asked by some non-conformist friends in the late 1830s to lead their temperance movement. It is clear to see from the friends and associates that were invited to stay at Greenbank that many of these visitors were free thinkers, not blinded by prejudice and became life long friends.

The reformers had become very concerned as to events in Ireland and they sent an invitation to Daniel O'Connell, the Irish leader known as the Liberator, to address a meeting in Liverpool. The invitation was accepted, his reply read:

Kitty Wilkinson

Daniel O'Connell, London, to William Rathbone, 20th March 1842.

Accepts an invitation of the leading reformers of Liverpool to attend a meeting to protest against the recent violation of the constitutional rights of a subject in the state trials in Ireland. He is glad the reformers of Liverpool are ready to join others in deploring the misgovernment of Ireland, in particular the mockery of law and justice in the state trials.

Daniel O'Connell was borne near Cahirciveen, Co Kerry Aug. 6, 1775 and was educated at English Colleges at St. Omar and Douai. He studied at Lincoln's Inn 1794-96 and was called to the Irish bar, in 1798.

Apart from Catholic emancipation Rathbone also involved himself with parliamentary reform, municipal reform, freedom of the West Indian slaves, the repeal of the Corn Laws, the penny postage scheme and national education. We also know he worked with his wife and Kitty Wilkinson to establish Public baths and wash-houses in Liverpool following the epidemic of 1832.

In 1868 The Liverpool Mercury wrote:

Mr. Rathbone and his party threw the Corporation Schools open under conditions which allowed all classes of religionists to share in the benefits that they offered.

He took part in the establishment of the Royal Institution. The Mechanics (which later became the Liverpool Institute) also owed much to his support. He also gave encouragement to Saturday Evening Concerts as a means of providing entertainment for people of the town and regularly attended himself. With Mr James Aiken and others he helped to found the Sailors' Home. The Liverpool Mercury wrote:

The extent of his private charity none ever knew, for he was emphatically a man to do good by stealth.

10

Thomas and Kitty
1846-1856

Thomas Wilkinson, was a humble and hard working man who appeared to live his life helping other people and must have felt very proud when, in 1846, he and Kitty were appointed Superintendents of the Corporation Baths. At last the Wilkinsons were enjoying some of the fruits of life. Kitty and Thomas showed the same level of commitment working in the new establishment as they did in 1832 when fighting the cholera, being paid for serving the community was like a bonus.

They no longer had the burden of looking after a family. Mrs Seward had passed on, but the painful memories of Kitty losing her youngest son still lingered. John the sea going son, was married with a family living in Stockport and the last of her orphans had gone to make their way in life. However they still had their friends and the friendship and respect of William Rathbone and his family. The Unitarian Church still played a big part in their lives which helped to fill the void in their much slower life despite the responsibilities of running the new Corporation Baths.

Many changes with improvements and amenities were taking place in the town much to Kitty's delight. She would surely have been pleased when Doctor Duncan was appointed to be Liverpool's first 'Medical Officer of Health' in 1846 shortly after her own appointment.

Just a few months later the first Borough Engineer Mr. James Newlands was appointed and took up his post in February 1847. This appointment brought about sewers, a better drainage system and the first connection of house drains to sewers. This made possible the substitution of water-closets for the privies and middens which we now know contributed so much to disease.

The new baths and washhouse was packed every day with women doing their family washing, many of them coming from other areas. This facility allowed people to do their washing in comfort with no restriction on the amount of water used. The wash-house also brought a comradeship amongst women which allowed them to express their feelings. It allowed them to escape from the drudgery of bad housing provided by private landlords and a chance to get away from husbands and children for a few hours.

Domestic servants from big houses also made use of the facilities for their employers. Many wealthy people living in the town would not have had facilities as good as those provided at the wash-house. What Kitty had created in her home in 1832 was to be repeated in every major town throughout the British Isles and many countries in Europe. In Scotland the wash-houses became known as "steamies".

The joy and pleasure the Wilkinsons derived from seeing people improve their lives, did not last long. People were fleeing the famine in Ireland and landing in the town from every type of vessel. We may never know for sure if Kitty played a part in helping to ease the suffering of the famine victims. However it would be hard to imagine she did not involve herself. Many victims of the famine would have used the wash-house and lived alongside her. It is more than possible that Kitty would have taken some new arrivals into her home, after all she had been caring for her neighbours most of her life.

Kitty had been greatly encouraged in her devotion to the community by Thomas since their marriage. He was the man behind a great woman. However sadly less than two years after his appointment of joint superintendent of the wash-house, Thomas took ill at home in 70 Upper Frederick Street with bronchitis. Kitty's son John was home from sea and staying with the family at the time. Thomas (*Note: John De-Monte was the informant at the time of death on 31 December, 1849. Also the name Demontee had been changed to De-monte.*) never recovered from his illness and died 31 December 1849.

Not for the first time in her life Kitty was alone. The man who had been by her side through one of the blackest periods in Liverpool's history was laid to rest in St. James Cemetery. The grave is listed as No. 209d but the headstone has long gone from the grave. Two weeks after Thomas died, the Rev. J.H. Thom in a sermon to his congregation spoke about the life of Thomas Wilkinson:

Pure religion, undefiled before God and the Father to visit the fatherless and widows of their affliction, and to keep himself unspotted from the world this poor man manifestly performed. Indeed the exact words of the Apostle do not equal the extent of his deeds. He did more than visit the fatherless and widow he made for them a home, and shared with them his own, the only limit to his bountiful charity was that which was occasioned by the accommodations of his narrow house.

The orphan child, homeless and helpless, he took to his own hearth; charged himself with its maintenance; helped it, when the time came, to some honest employment; and never lost sight of it till it was able to thrive by its own industry. In this way, in the course of a not lengthened life, as many as forty-five have found in him a father, been cherished, clothed. fed, educated, and pushed into the world.

Many a sailor lad, on distant seas, has no thought of home but this poor man's house, and whenever he returns to port, brings to the parents who adopted him the offering of his gratitude. In speaking with him I have sometimes been perplexed, for an instinct of modesty and nobleness he never spoke of these children as orphans, but always as if they belonged to himself and were his own children.

When those children grew fit for labour, and, equal to their own support, found their dwelling elsewhere, and had their place supplied by other orphans in this good man's house, he kept over them a watchful eye; and fearful least they might forfeit their place by any neglect, he, summer and winter, before the earliest call to labour, made daily his morning round to see that they were roused, and that neither weariness nor over labour, natural heaviness, or accidental infirmity, detained them from their work.

I have ascertained that for twenty years, in all weathers, at all seasons, in cold and wet, in the darkness of mid-winter as in the softness of the summer's dawn, this man left his own house a full hour before the six o' clock bell, not only to summon the children of his adoption, but to do the same office for many others who, through illness in their family, or weakness and exhaustion in themselves, were dependent on his vigilance.

This is true Christian, and it shows how rich the world is in the opportunities of good; that everywhere there is room for

*those fine qualities of patience, and trust, and self-denial,
and heroism, which in a more exalted scene would draw the
admiration of mankind.*

*Whosoever shall give to one of those little ones a cup of
cold water only, verily I say unto you he shall in no way lose
his reward.*

Kitty continued in her post at the Corporation Baths and
Washhouse until the 23rd August 1852, when the Council felt she
should retire. Kitty had reached the age of sixty-six and was
retired without a pension and given four weeks pay in lieu of
notice. However two years later in 1854, efforts were made to
secure a pension.

A report by Borough Engineer James Newlands to the Liverpool
Town Council in 1856 praised the work of Kitty Wilkinson.,

*In 1832 when cholera ravaged the town, the necessity of
cleanliness as a means of arresting or abating the plague became
apparent, but poor families huddled, healthy and sick together,
often in an underground cellar without the means for personal
cleanliness, and still less for washing their clothes and bedding,
thus nothing could be done by them to prevent the spreading of the
infection.*

*It was left to one of their own class and station, a Mrs. Catherine
Wilkinson, of Frederick Street, Liverpool, to provide a remedy.
She, the wife of a labourer. living in one of the worst and most
crowded streets of the town, allowed her poorer neighbours who
were destitute of the means of heating water, to wash their clothes
in the back kitchen of her humble abode, and to dry them in the
covered passage and backyard belonging to it.*

*Aided by the District Provident Society, and some benevolent
ladies, this courageous self-denying woman contrived to provide
for the washing of, on an average, 85 families per week. This,*

Kitty Wilkinson

began during the visitation of the cholera, and continued for several years; the poor people contributing 1d, per week to assist in defraying the expenses. The great supporters of Mrs. Wilkinson in her praiseworthy efforts were Mr and Mrs. William Rathbone. To their fostering care we owe the recognition of her services, and the institutions to which they give rise. Here, then, was the germ of public washhouse institutions called into existence as a means of palliating a great evil.

Upper Frederick Street

Upper Frederick Street, September 25 1925

Upper Frederick Street

131

First Public Washhouse Rebuilt in 1853

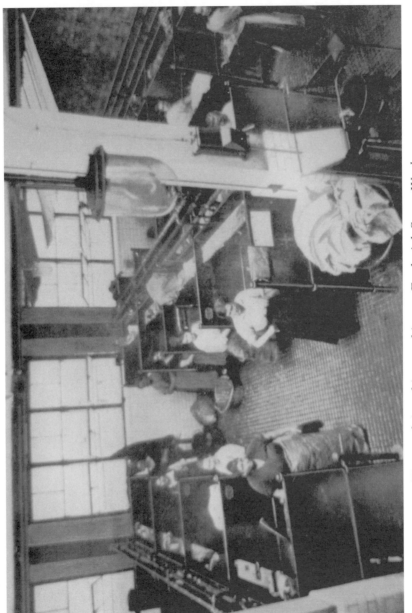

Women doing thier washing at Frederick Street Washouse

Frederick Street Washhouse

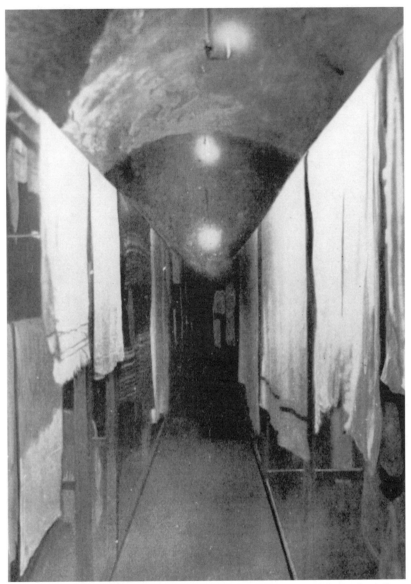

Interior of underground drying chamber in the old Frederick Street washhouse, 1925, just before the transfer

Frederick Street washhouse drying room in the 1925 establishment

'Kitty Wilkinson' baths and washhouse, 1925, wash stall and equipment

Private bath

11

Life without Thomas

As late as 1858 there was still a reluctance by those who sat on the council to build more wash-houses in Liverpool. The town by this time had expanded its boundaries, and people where still pouring in looking for work. The charities were doing their best, but were not in a position to rehouse people, however well meaning their efforts. Only legislation could bring more permanent changes. The District Provident Society did all they could with limited funds, but nevertheless they played a vital part in trying to alleviate the suffering.

In spite of all the pioneering work done by Kitty Wilkinson the housing situation and water supply was still in a bad state. She had given a lead in caring for the poor, had shown the world her nursing skills, and influenced William Rathbone in his pioneering work in the nursing profession. Education was also uppermost in Kitty's mind. She indicated the need for education among the working class and again led by example in passing on her skills. Kitty by this time was seventy-two and Thomas was no longer there to comfort her. Upper Frederick Street was filled every day with people passing Kitty's front door on their way to the wash-house.

Kitty Wilkinson

In 1858 a book was published titled, "Twelve Lectures to The Men Of Liverpool" by Hugh Stowell Brown. One lecture was titled, "Cleanliness is next to Godliness," wherein the influence of Kitty is apparent even though she is not actually named. Extracts give a clear picture of conditions in 1858:

> *Now, as to the importance of physical cleanliness here is a rather startling fact to begin with. In England alone the average annual number of deaths from disease is about 300,000 while the number of deaths from physical decay, by the progress of time, is only 35,000 that is to say, only about one person in ten dies through causes strictly natural, and absolutely unavoidable. Most certainly there is, and the chief cause is, beyond all question, dirt, dirty skins, dirty clothes, dirty houses, dirty gutters, and a dirty atmosphere.*

People living in the Frederick Street area must have looked on Kitty in amazement living to such an age in spite of the foul sanitary conditions in and around Frederick Street. The next extract shows clearly the early death rate amongst young people:

> *A few years ago it was shown that the average life span in Liverpool was only 17 years, and the life of the operative classes was no more than 15 years. The study of the bills of mortality shows that such an appalling loss of life is mainly due to the absence of cleanliness, and the presence of dirt. An eminent physician, Dr. Guy, says deficient drainage, if not the parent, is certainly the nurse, of fever. My own opinion is, that fever is a contagious disease, spreading from person just like small-pox or scarlet fever and, like those diseases, haunts crowded or ill-drained districts, It loves the banks of rivers, the borders of marshes, the edges of stagnant pools. It makes itself a home in the neighbourhood of cess pools and badly constructed drains.*

It has a perfect horror of fresh air, soap, and whitewash; and when left to itself will linger for years amid scenes of filth and corruption.

In this next extract of Hugh Stowell Brown's Lectures, slow change in providing decent housing conditions is quite apparent. It is almost thirty years after the 1832 cholera outbreak and little has changed in the provision of housing.

In the few minutes you take to walk from St. Giles's to St. George's, Bloomsbury, in the Metropolis you may not be aware that you have almost passed from life unto death; but such is the fact; for in the former district, which is very crowded and dirty, though, so far as I have inspected it, nothing like so filthy as many parts of Liverpool, the poor people in those narrow courts and dark cellars live only 17 years; whilst in the latter district, which is open and well-built, with squares, large houses, good drainage, the inhabitants live on average to the age of forty. What differences does it make whether a man lives in St. Giles's or St. George's? Only that in the latter region he will probably live 23 years longer.

Hugh Stowell Brown sees the need for every household to be liberally supplied with running water. He also blames the denial of running water as the main cause of disease and for whatever reason no one should be denied it.

Health is only enjoyment to the rich, it is the very existence to the poor so therefore everything that the working man can do to secure this, he ought to do. To secure it, the first requisites are soap and water; a clean skin is absolutely essential to sound and vigorous health; whatever it costs the town, water ought to be liberally supplied to every working man's house, so that every morning before he goes to work, and every night when he goes home, he may have a good wash.

The Corporation have done good service in providing public baths and wash houses and this is one of the best things that they have ever done; a matter of far greater practical utility than the building of St. George's Hall. If a working man has twopence to spare on a Saturday night, the best public house [Washhouse or slipper baths] he can go to is situated in Cornwallis Street; or if he lives in the north end, he will find one in Paul Street. I wish there were so many more, one at least in every ward in the borough; and I believe there will be some day, when the public mind is fully alive to the fact, that, cleanliness is next to godliness, and that the water-shop is far and away better than the gin-shop, as health is better than disease, plenty better than poverty, and life better than death.

Stowell Brown shows his concern for the working man and slow but steady progress being made in housing provision and closing of cellars.

What shall we say of the working man's dwelling? I am afraid that, with every precaution, there must be dirt and disease, unless a better class of house, better situated, be provided for the people. There certainly has been some improvement effected of later years.

Many of those cellars, which are no better than preparatory graves, (they cannot even be called, in the language of the Necropolis, 'tidy graves') have been shut up are, at all events no longer used as human habitations it was quite right to put a stop to such a nuisance.

The owners of such properties have no moral right to let

them for such purposes; to let a cellar or a house that is unhealthy is as great a crime as to sell putrid meat. The result of closing the wretched cellars soon showed itself. I have no recent data at hand but perhaps the statistics of 1849 the year of the cholera are as useful as any other. Near the end of that year, 4,700 cellars had been cleared of 20,000 people; and one of the cellar districts, lost only 94 in the cholera of 1849 which, in a previous epidemic had lost 500 inhabitants.

I submit that it is sinful to build houses which common sense proves cannot avoid being the abodes of filth. If a man is going to build houses he is morally bound to deliver them to the tenant in a sanitary state; you would execrate him if he let·the houses in such condition that they were liable to fall in a gale of wind. But if this builder of Jerry houses says - " I cannot afford to build healthy houses;" well, then, in the name of all that's honest and humane, don't build at all. If a butcher or a fishmonger says, "I cannot afford to sell wholesome beef or wholesome mackerel," I say, well, then, shut up, and take to some other trade; if you cannot feed the people, that's no reason why you should poison them; and if you, Jerry builder cannot shelter the people wholesomely, don't attempt to shelter them at all.

It is clear from the above that all improvements Kitty worked so hard for were now being called for by others. It was many years after those lectures that any serious attempt was made to improve the lives of townspeople. The Sanitary Amendment Act of 1854 gave the Town Council powers to compel owners to connect house drains to main sewers. But absence of an adequate water supply held up conversion of privies into water-closets. It was not until 1860 when the health committee adopted a policy of rejecting plans which did not have provision for water closets that any real action on that front took place. It was not until 1866 that most conversions had been carried out - 34 years after the first cholera epidemic.

Kitty must have been very saddened at this slow pace of progress, and yet some landlords still opposed installation of the water closet. Landlords even blamed any new out-break of disease on new sanitary provisions. One councillor even thought the health committee were wrong in coming between landlord and tenant, by taking responsibility away from the tenant.

The medical officer of health was attacked by people who did not live in working class districts, saying conversions were ordered without any fixed rules, but instead on the personal opinion of the medical officer. They believed a privy was prejudicial to health. However, the good work of the town's medical officer was having an effect on views of other officials in the town. This can be seen in a report of the Engineer and Chief Superintendent of Baths and wash-houses. This shows concern for feelings, of people who were worse off than others.

The question arises, are the very poor attracted or repelled by the existing establishments? The Engineer and Chief Superintendent are inclined to think that, so far as grown-up people are concerned, the very poor do not care to come into contact with those who are better clothed and in more fortunate circumstances, therefore the existing establishments, having only one entrance and one ticket window for all classes, are such as would deter the very poor from using the baths.

It is found by experience that the majority of people who have to walk from a quarter to half-a-mile for a bath do not use the baths. If those poor people have to be cleansed, then the means of doing so must be taken, as to were, to their own doors. Very careful consideration must be given as to the best method of carrying out the work, so as to make the residents in the very poor districts habitual bathers from choice, and not by compulsion. To many of the uneducated, the word bath seems to strike them with terror, and taking a bath is looked upon by them as a punishment.

By the provision of small establishments in the centre of densely populated slum districts, for cleansing purposes only, the Corporation would be providing the means of doing a real good. It is not essential that these establishments should be luxurious; they ought to be unpretentious, yet substantial, clean, and inviting, and thus those persons for whom they are intended ought not to be deterred from making good use of them.

The Baths and Wash-house Committee had become very advanced in its methods by this time. Through the introduction of shower cubicles to the people's baths, they could provide more facilities.

The rain and spray cabin has a portion of its floor depressed, so as to form a foot-bath, the overflow of which is fixed at such a height as to allow the water to cover the bather's ankles. This allows the bather to thoroughly soap himself, and to wash his feet before using the warm rain bath, or ring shower. The ring shower, which is the chief feature of the system, is placed overhead, and is formed in a circular ring, so that the water does not strike the bather's head, but falls in a gentle shower on his shoulders.

As the body is cleansed, so the dirt is carried down to the feet and into the drain. When the bather is thoroughly cleansed, by the manipulation of a lever the temperature of the water can be reduced to suit. A spray or needle is fixed at one side of the cabin, whereby the bather may enjoy its tonic effects. An ascending warm spray is fixed in one corner, for washing the lower portions of the body.

Apart from its lower cost and economy of space, the rain bath possesses many advantages over the ordinary slipper bath, viz., its perfect simplicity, certain cleanliness is insured, all risk of infection or contagion avoided, less danger of taking cold after use, the tonic effect of the spray on the skin is valuable, stimulating the skin, thus protecting the bather from subsequent exposure. There is also an immense saving of water and fuel; an ordinary slipper bath consumes no less than 50 gallons of water; the time occupied by a bather is considerably less, and there is no danger of drowning.

Bain baths are, from a cleansing point of view, undoubtedly the baths of the future.

The slipper bath of to-day may well, in its way, act not only as an antidote for colds, rheumatism, and other complaints, but as a cleansing apparatus it does not bear comparison with the rain bath. Take, as an example a coalheaver, or other workmen engaged in a dirty occupation. On leaving off work he ought to be able to obtain, at a small cost, a thorough cleansing before going home.

In the event of his taking a warm slipper bath (for which he must pay 2d) he washes the dirt off his body and bathes in it. In the rain bath (which ought to be obtainable for one penny) as the bather washes the dirt off the body, the dirt is carried away in the drain, leaving the bather perfectly cleansed.

News of the 'Kitty Wilkinson Baths and Wash-house' and the

part Liverpool played in its development had long since reached the rest of the country. Officials from other towns were sent to inspect what was taking place in Liverpool and adopted the baths and washhouse system. The Edinburgh Authorities had attached a nursery to each of their Public Wash-houses.

In Germany from about 1870, an active movement for the establishment of "Peoples Baths" was carried on. The subject was brought to the notice of the German Public Health Association in Berlin, in 1886, by Dr Occar Lasser, Professor of Skin Diseases at the University of Berlin. It was chiefly through action taken by Dr Lasser that the great advance in the provisions of cleansing facilities for the poor on the continent had taken place. In Austria, at Vienna, the first public baths was opened in the year 1888.

Some 'States' of America sent eminent people to Britain to inspect the baths. People's baths were erected at Yonkers, New York, Buffalo, Boston, Brooklyn, Mass, Philadelphia, Chicago, and many other cities. What had started off as an act of kindness and Christian duty by Kitty Wilkinson in Liverpool, resulted in eminent people from all over the world writing papers on the advantages of peoples baths, for the sake of the well being of their own people.

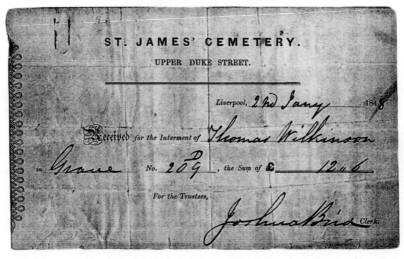

Interment of Thomas Wilkinson, St. James Cemetery

12

The Final Years

Gore's Street Directory in 1858 listed Kitty as a boarding house keeper at 70, Upper Frederick Street. She was living just a few doors from the "The Kitty Wilkinson Baths and Wash-house" which was still serving the community. People were still passing Kitty's door with their bundles of dirty washing perched on their heads. If they were lucky, they would have some sort of contraption on wheels to carry the washing. Not many poor women would have had use of a pram for their babies, so chances of having an old pram would have been very remote. Kitty would have observed the women a few hours later returning with their clean clothes and bedding.

Almost thirty years had passed since the first signs of cholera had brought death and misery to the area. The name of Kitty Wilkinson would mean very little to those people arriving in the town after 1850. People were still arriving from Wales, Ireland, Scotland and surrounding areas of Lancashire and Cheshire.

In 1859 Kitty's health was a cause for concern, long gone were the orphans and lodgers. John her son was married and had moved away from Frederick Street to live in Stockport. It is possible he was at sea during this time. Kitty was not too well at the beginning of the year and went to convalesce at the home of Mrs Gilbertson. On her return home, Kitty composed a short letter to Mrs Gilbertson. It is clear from reading the letter that Kitty's mind and intellect were very much intact, although her health was failing.

Liverpool Feb 2nd 1859

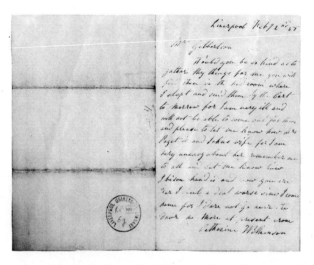

Letter written by Kitty to Mrs Gilbertson, Feb 2, 1869

Mrs Gilbertson

Would you be so kind as to gather my things for me you will find them in the bedroom where I slept and send them by the Cart tomorrow for I am very ill and will not be able to come out for them, and please to let me know how Mrs. Paget is and Johns wife for I am very uneasy about her, remember me to all and let me know how Ibison hand is and how you are For I feel a deal worse since I came home for I dare not go near the door no more at present from.

Catherine Wilkinson

The letter goes on to inquire about John's wife, Kitty's daughter in-law. Kitty also inquires about Mrs. Paget, daughter of William Rathbone. The letter also indicates she had written many letters in the past. Despite her illness, Kitty did not appear to labour with the content of the letter. However towards the end of it you can get the feel of Kitty's tortured mind and lonely circumstance.

Kitty must also have kept records of her housekeeping, being the organised woman that she was. Thomas her husband at one time kept a coal cellar (a coal dealer). Thomas could not read or write, so it would have been up to Kitty to do the book keeping.

By 1860 the town that adopted Kitty, was no longer a tiny little seaport, standing on a river that flows down to the Irish Sea. The same river which had brought Kitty to the town like a guardian angel, after she had done battle with a raging sea on leaving her home in Derry. She was like a great salmon fighting against a raging tide making its way up stream, as though nature had programmed her to make her way to a town that was in need of her courage and humanity.

She must have watched in wonderment the steamers that were replacing the sailing ships leaving for almost every port in Ireland, sailing to Dublin, Wexford, Waterford, Cork and in the north, Drogeda, Dundalk and Newry. There were lines to Belfast and Derry, and on the west coast to Sligo, Westport, Ballina, Limerick and banks of the Shannon.

However for all the steam ships that could have taken her back home, Kitty never left the town she loved so well. Many of the orphans that she had cared for would be merchant seamen in the steamers sailing for America, Europe, Africa and Austraila and the rest of the world.

The population of the City of Liverpool was still growing, the port having become the main route for embarkation to America.

However there were those who found that they did not have the financial means to get them to the United States of America, so they joined the ranks of the people who settled in the town.

Many years had passed since Kitty Wilkinson had shown the way with hygiene, her nursing skills, which had been self taught, and the venture into education when she was a young woman just after she was released from bondage in the mills. Also there were the orphans that she had fed, nursed back to health and saved from an early death on the streets. Her life was spent like a great fisherman casting her net to pull in all those who needed her. Liverpool and the rest of the country were slow to take up what Kitty had started in 1832. Only two Wash-houses had been built by the local Council, along with three public bathing establishments by 1860, but once they did many changes were to take place.

After the building of the first washhouse in Frederick Street, came a second at Paul Street, just off Vauxhall Road. The Paul-Street Baths, were also built by the Corporation, and were constructed of brick in the Elizabethan style. There are plunge baths for both males and females, with 34 separate baths, and four vapour baths. The private baths were of slate, with the exception of three, in the upper story, of white marble, for which three different prices were charged. At the rear of these Baths, and separated by a yard was the Paul Street Wash-house. That was also separated from a building used for washing infected clothing.

The third of these, was the Cornwallis Street Baths, off Duke Street, near Liverpool City centre. The baths consisted of three large plunge baths (2 pence and 3 pence, first class) and numerous separate baths. The terms of admission for bathers was.....1d., 3d., and 6p., for cold baths, and 2p., 6p., to 1s., for warm baths.

They were, at the time, described as, useful and agreeable baths used by upwards of 100,000 persons yearly.

Frederick Street had the "Kitty Wilkinson Wash-house" but no bathing facilities. So despite improvements in sanitation and flushing lavatories, bathing facilities were still hard to come by. Even washing infected clothes in a safe controlled area was not a priority with the council, Upper Frederick Street and Paul Street being the only two.

However the salt water baths, at 'St. George's Pierhead,' had been in existence since 1825. This establishment contained a gentlemen's plunge bath and a ladies' plunge bath together with suites of private baths, both cold and hot. "The water used is carefully filtered through gravel beds, and is beautifully clear." The baths were built at a cost of £27,772, and were used by between 40,000 to 50,000 persons yearly. As the years went by things did get a little better as bathing and wash-houses were built in the town and in many other towns throughout the land. In Liverpool in 1859 Thomas Baines wrote:

Up to the year 1848, Liverpool had the evil reputation of being the most unhealthy town in the kingdom; nearly every year it was scourged by typhus fever, and other diseases arising from impure air, bad drainage, damp houses, and bad diet.

Since that time the whole town has been re-drained and re-sewered at a cost of upwards of £200,000, many hundred thousand pounds have been expended in bringing in an additional supply of water from a distance of between twenty and thirty miles. The lowest class of the population have been compelled to abandon the wretched cellars in which they formerly lived, and the most unremitting care has been exercised in removing every nuisance dangerous to the public health.

Immense results have already been achieved; and, though

153

Kitty Wilkinson

much remains to be done, the efforts to effect it never cease.

Kitty's life at this time was slowly ebbing away, the strength of this great woman was leaving her body, like the sap leaving a great tree, alone in a forest. Gone were the sea of faces that had passed through her hands, the orphans and the sick, whom she nursed and guided through life. There was no great newspaper correspondent writing to the "Times" to tell the world about this most wonderful woman. It was left to the Liverpool Newspapers to inform the rest of the country that it was Kitty Wilkinson, who fought the cholera almost single handed, until she was helped in her task by Mr. and Mrs. Rathbone. Her work amongst the poor must have planted the seeds of progress into the minds of other men and women from other towns and other countries.

Kitty Wilkinson died on the 11 November, 1860, and present at the time of her death was a friend of Kitty, Mary Lawson. Mary could not write her own name, the death certificate gave the mark of Mary Lawson of 39 Jordan Street.

An obituary appeared in The Liverpool Mercury Tuesday November 13, 1860:

Death of Catherine Wilkinson,

The Originator Of The Wash-House.

This humble but not unknown philanthropist died on Saturday last, at the age of 73; and a highly respected correspondent has sent us the following of the deceased a tribute to her memory emanating from one who has an instinctive appreciation of all that is good and generous:-
"It maybe well for those of small means, as well as for those more largely endowed, occasionally to review the respective responsibilities of the position in which they are placed and to take note of what might be accomplished with very small

means but with a very large heart."

This was eminently the case in the humble individual whose death this day we record. The good seed was sown at a very early age by her attendance upon an infirm old lady while going her rounds to relieve the sickness and the sorrows of the poor. The seed fell upon the ground and produced an abundant harvest through her long and useful life, during which her poor neighbours were always sure of her sympathy and advice and such aid as her small means but self-sacrificing energy could make available. As to her own necessities, which so circumstanced, must often have been pleasing, she was remarkably unrequiring and reserved.

During the eventful season of the cholera in this town her efforts (fearless of risk to herself) were unceasing both by day and by night and they were rendered the more valuable by her practical knowledge and inventive power to meet emergencies as they arose. It was during this period that she originated, in her own cellar, the plan for wash-houses for the poor, which have since been so generally adopted. Though labouring for her daily bread, yet she and her husband (who died some years before her) at different times received many orphans into her dwelling with no claim upon on them but their destitution, taking charge of them with parental care until able to support themselves, or otherwise provided for. In a truly Samaritan and Christian spirit her efforts to relieve knew no limit but in her power to serve. The widow's mite was not infrequently all of this world's wealth which she had to give."

Kitty was interred on Wednesday November 14 1860 at St. James Cemetery. Present were William Rathbone and many of her adopted children. However her son John Demontee was not in attendance. It could be that word of his mother's death had not reached him at his home in Stockport. We know that John was a seaman so it is possible that he was on the high seas. It was of course possibe that John had died before his mother. Mr. Shimming of Pit Street made arrangements for the funeral

In its obituary column Gores General Advertiser November 22, 1860 reported the death of Catherine Wilkinson. "The inventor of Wash-Houses for the poor."

Just over seven years after the death of Kitty, Mr. William Rathbone, the man who had played such a vital role in the work of Kitty Wilkinson died February 1st, 1868 aged 80 years. He died at his home, Greenbank, Liverpool, and was buried at Smithdown Lane Cemetery. After his death, a statue of him was erected by public subscription in Sefton Park Liverpool. His wife Margaret survived him by fifteen years.

Record of Baptisms of John and Joseph Emanuel

13

In Honour of Kitty Wilkinson

Almost fifty years had passed since Kitty died but her memory was still alive. In 1909, at a meeting of the Liverpool Corporation Baths Committee, a letter was read from Mr. Theodore F. S. Tinnie son of the first chairman of the Baths Committee. Mr. Tinnie was no longer a resident of Liverpool and was living at Hawkhurst, Kent. Enclosed were photographs of Catherine Wilkinson and attached to the back of Kitty's photograph was a copy of a memorandum.

She was the wife of a labourer who, although she died in 1860 she should still be recalled by Liverpool people as a foremost heroine of the city. Mrs. Wilkinson, who was the pioneer of baths and wash-houses, was known in Kent, as "Kitty of Liverpool." A photograph of Catherine Wilkinson called "Kitty of Liverpool" (see Chamber's Miscellany) and the originator of public baths and wash-houses.

She was born in Derry, in Ireland, on the 24th October, 1785. Her father's name was Seaward, her mother's name Mitchell, both perished at different times at sea, the latter off Hoyle Bank, with another infant daughter, in 1790, and "Kitty" was saved. Her early life was spent in the poorer districts, until her marriage in 1812. She was twice married, first to De monte a sailor, who was wrecked and drowned, secondly to Wilkinson, who died the 31st December, 1847.

The latter and "Kitty" had charge of the first "Baths and Wash-house," in Upper Frederick Street, Liverpool. "Kitty" had only one child of her own by her first husband, but very many adopted orphans have learned to call her "mother." She died on the 11th November, 1860, aged 75 years.

Indefatigable and self-sacrificing,
She was the widow's friend,
The support of the orphan,
The fearless and unwearied nurse of the sick.

"For they all did cast, in of their abundance, but she of her want did cast in all that she had, even all her living." St. Mark, 11th chapter, 14th verse.

In 1909 an article in the Liverpool Daily Post and Mercury informs us that:

It is rarely that we have enfolded to us such a chapter of sublime heroism and philanthropy as that disclosed in the humble life of Kitty Wilkinson, and we do hope, for the sake of the magnificent example which she presents to women of all ranks and classes of society, as well as for the claims to remembrance which her labours constitute upon the community she nobly served, that the citizens of Liverpool will numerously and generously combine to provide some tangible and suitable memorial which shall serve to remind future generations of what she was and what she did.

In another article The Liverpool Daily Post and Mercury, of 16 March, 1909 informs us of Kitty Wilkinson:

The South Corporation Infants' School arose from a number of children she had collected in her bedroom, whose parents were ill of cholera.

The year after this editorial appeared in the paper, The Life of Kitty Wilkinson a Lancashire Heroine. by Winefrede R. Rathbone, was published.

Kitty's image was later engraved in "The Staircase Window" in the Lady Chapel of the Liverpool Cathedral and can be seen on descending the steps into the Chapel.

Sixty-six years after the death of Kitty, the City of Liverpool decided to honour her once more and, during Civic Week October 1926 Miss Marie Lohr, a great actress of her day was asked to play the lead in a pageant to be performed at the Gilbert Street Wash House.

Marie Lohr, an Australian actress who was born in 1890 and had appeared in most of London's theatres, was asked if she would play the part of Kitty Wilkinson in the pageant. Two other actresses, Miss Muriel Randel, and Miss Diane Wynyard, who were appearing, in "The Love Game" at the Shakespeare Theatre were also asked to take part, they all agreed. 'The Evening Express' of Liverpool reported on the pageant:

The Opening of the first Public Baths and Wash-House, in Frederick Street. The Boy's Brigade will line the enclosure. Kitty Wilkinson (Miss Marie Lohr) and her companions will meet in the wash-house at 11 o'clock accompanied by a selection of music by Bibby's Band. Two boys will bring two forms out of the wash-house, and place them in position and eight boys and eight girls will sit on the forms.

When the band ceases playing a call will be sounded on trumpets, 'Kitty Wilkinson' preceded by a small boy and girl, will leave the 'Kitty Wilkinson' wash-house, Gilbert

Kitty Wilkinson

Miss Marie Löhr as 'Kitty Wilkinson' assisted by Miss Murial Randall and Miss Diana Wynyard. Civic Week 1926

Miss Marie Löhr as 'Kitty Wilkinson'
Civic Week 1926

Kitty Wilkinson

Street at 11,30, am. The Lord Mayor and the Lady Mayoress will drive up, and on alighting they will shake hands with 'Kitty Wilkinson.' Kitty will then give a lesson to the class, eulogising the life and character of the noble woman, after which they rise and will sing the old folk song, 'Dashing Away with a Smoothing Iron.'

As the singing is finishing two working women (Miss Muriel Randall and Miss Diane Wynyard) leaving the baths carrying baskets of unwashed linen will walk up to Kitty and place them on the ground in front of her. The Lord Mayor and Lord Derby will address the gathering. The Lady Mayoress will then make a short speech. As my predecessor of old presented in 1846 to Kitty Wilkinson a silver tea-set, I have now the pleasure to present to you a miniature replica inscribed as follows: Presented to Kitty Wilkinson (Miss Marie Lohr) by the Lady Mayoress (Mrs. E. W. Hope) - Civic Week Pageant October, 1926.

Archdeacon G. F. Howson in a letter to the Liverpool Express October 1926, expressed his feelings for Kitty's memory:

I have been wondering whether in civic week preparation a small but not insignificant piece of commemoration could be achieved. The grave of Kitty Wilkinson in St. James Cemetery, is strangely neglected. Everybody's business is nobody's. Still, perhaps the trustees of the cemetery might deal with it by cutting the words, clearing the weeds and putting the stone upright I dare say they would if they thought of it. Perhaps this suggestion may reach, I hope so.

Archdeacon Howson's letter came to the notice of the trustees and the grave was attended to. Kitty was again to be honoured in 1927 by the City of Liverpool. The Liverpool Daily Post and Mercury, reported the following:

In Honour of Kitty Wilkinson

The memory of Kitty Wilkinson, the heroic woman of humble birth, who performed great public service by the institution of wash-houses in Liverpool during the cholera plague of 1832, will be more firmly held in admiration as a result of a gift-book scheme which the Lord Mayor (Mr. F. C. Bowring) has offered to finance.   By this scheme a book of the life of Kitty Wilkinson will be presented annually in every senior girls school in the city.

The prize will be award to elementary school girls who, in the opinion of their teachers, have earnestly and successfully tried to carry out direction "Thou shalt love thy neighbour as thyself."

The book is edited by Mr. Herbert H. Rathbone, and published by Henry Young's at two shillings and sixpence.

Two thousand copies are to be reserved for sale, and from these there will be presented annually in every senior girls' school in the City a copy of the memoir to the girl most fit to receive it.

The Lord Mayor has generously offered to provide the funds necessary to carry out this suggestion. The Council of Education are to be asked to receive and hold the proceeds of the sale of the book to the public, with power to use such proceeds for the purpose of printing a fresh edition when the two thousand set aside for prizes are exhausted - that is in about ten years time.   Power will be given to the Council to use the money for other purposes, according to their discretion, as it is thought not wise to legislate in a matter of this kind too far ahead.

The prize-books will, it is suggested, bear the inscription.

Kitty Wilkinson

Kitty Wilkinson Prize,
instituted in the year 1927
by
The Lord Mayor of Liverpool
F. C. Bowring Esq. J. P.

A further tribute was paid to Kitty, by The Right Hon. T. P. O'Conner, M. P. P C who wrote, the foreword for the book.

I have been asked to write a Foreword to this extremely interesting little book. It requires, however no Foreword; its own pages, written though they be with restraint and simplicity, are alone sufficient to inspire countless readers. When in the recent civic week in Liverpool, I was asked to take part in the celebrations of Kitty Wilkinson's memory, I had to avow that I had been, up to a short time before, ignorant of her extraordinary achievements, though afterwards I dimly recollected that almost half a century ago I had read an article about her in some periodical.

The self-devotion of this woman instinctive, untaught, uninspired by anybody but her own brave and beautiful character - to the relief of suffering and want, is really almost an incredible story. She seems like some `hound of heaven,' to pursue misery, illness, suffering women, half starved children, wherever they might be hidden.

Joined to this Christian self-devotion there was really a genius for finding the practical means of combating great crisis. She may be described as the discoverer of the methods of fighting the terrible scourge of cholera when it came to Liverpool in 1832. It was she who first inspired the despairing and bereaved people around her with the new idea of avoiding infection by washing and purifying the clothes in which the victims had died.

Her only method of dealing with this terrible problem was a big boiler in her own tiny rooms in a miserable tenement; and there for weeks she slaved at this work, and managed to keep the disease from reaching the terrible dimensions which otherwise it would have attained. It was almost the instinct of genius to have invented this method.

I refer my readers to the following to learn the many details of this uninterrupted work of charity and beneficence in which Kitty Wilkinson was engaged all her life, and to discover the fact that she was never much higher than a factory hand and a charwoman. Finally, I am proud to say she was Irish by birth, though nearly all her life was spent among English people.

It is an additional recommendation of this book to me, that it is the work mainly, and possible wholly, of a member or members of the Rathbone family whose social work in Liverpool is as notable as that of Kitty Wilkinson, though performed in a different way and under different conditions."

In his wisdom T. P. O'Conner, describes Kitty, as living in a miserable tenement. However tenements were never located in Denison Street.

Two letters were received by the Liverpool Weekly Post in June 1927.

Dear Sir

I would like to thank you, for your mentioning Kitty Wilkinson's grave, in the Liverpool Weekly Post. My Mother took me to St. James Cemetery to show me that grave nearly fifty years ago, but after looking about for nearly 2 hours she could not find it. Or no trace of the stone that was upon it. She thought the Cemetery Authorities had moved it after being closed so long.

Thanking you again

I remain

Victor Demont.

Stockport   23/5/27

Dear Sir, i would like to thank you for your mentioning Kitty Wilkinsons, grave in the Liverpool Weekly Post. My mother took me to Saint James Cemetery to show me that grave nearly 50 years ago but after looking about for nearly 2 hours She could not find it, nor no trace of the Stone that was upon it. She thought the Cemetery authorities had moved after being closed so long .

Thanking you again

I remain

Victor Demount

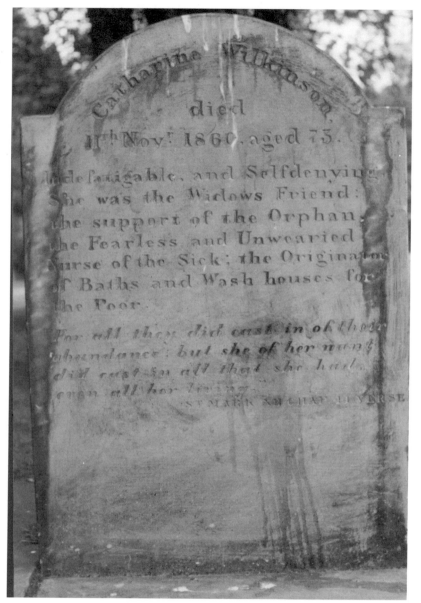

Kitty's Headstone

Kitty Wilkinson

27 Weble Lane Hair Street, Stockport

3rd June 1927.

Dear Sir

I am sorry I did not send my address, I am sending you an old grave paper and you can see the difference between burying then and now.

Yours Sincerely

Victor E Demont.

On August the 20, 1927 the Weekly Post published the contents of a meeting between, C. A. Healey, and grandson of Kitty.

A few days ago I had the privilege of speaking to a grandson of the illustrious Kitty Wilkinson, whose name is written in golden letters across the door-steps of every hospital and nursing home in the world. His name is Victor Demont, and he is a sturdy, stalwart middle-aged man of sixty eight years working in a Redditch Mill, just as his great ancestor worked in another when she was a mere child of eleven.

In Honour of Kitty Wilkinson

He showed me some treasured relics of the great and wonderful Kitty, the cream jug and the tea-service presented to her in 1846 by the two Queens, Victoria and Charlotte. By the Countess of Derby, and the Ladies of Liverpool. The presentation was made twelve years after the event. That cream jug is now in the keeping of Mr. Robert Gladstone, president of the society of Lovers of Old Liverpool.

I am tracing the whereabouts of the rest of the service so that our President (for I am privileged to be the secretary of that unique society which has Mr. T.P. O'Conner, Sir Leslie Scott, and Mr. Jack Hayes as its vice-presidents) may hand it to the Lord Mayor for exhibition during Civic Week.

I have been reading some of the literature written about that great and amazing woman, and when I think of the religious gnats who buzzed about her and tried to sting her into their own narrow groove, then I marvel all the more that this grand glorious woman went steadily on her way, knowing that there were no banners no coloured regiments in God's army of service, she did her work greatly fearing no reward or reproof.

A tea service presented by the two queens and a host of wealthy ladies might well intoxicate the head of a woman who looked with reverence upon earthy rank. I do not suppose that Kitty Wilkinson ever had two cups of tea out of that service.

She had no time for vanity, brave heart right to her dying day, she was ever working and now I do believe she is ever on the move throughout heaven with a duster. She had two children by her first husband, Manual De Monte, and had children by her second husband Thomas Wilkinson, who died their father following them soon to their fruitless grave.

Yet her first marriage has prospered to a second, a third and even a fourth generation. Mr. De Monte lives in a quiet little suburb of Stockport, works in a Redditch Mill, and at the age of sixty-eight is younger than men of half his years. He has an enthusiasm and a vim well worthy of the stock from which he has sprung, and he has an intense love of Liverpool well worthy of the great Kitty Wilkinson.

He told me a pathetic story. Fifty years ago his mother and himself made a pilgrimage to Liverpool to see the grave in St. James's Cemetery in which lies all that is mortal of the founder of public baths and wash-houses, night schools, kindergartens, mechanics Institutes, and the art of nursing, whether in the home or the hospital. Neither the daughter-in-law nor the grandson could find the grave.

It was rescued from its obscurity by Archdeacon Howson just a year and a half ago, and now, thanks to his loving care, the grave has become a shrine outside Liverpool's beautiful Cathedral.

The tea service presented to Kitty, (which was reported to be somewhere in Liverpool) was not found. Only the silver cream jug was in the safe keeping of Mr. De Monte, Kitty's grandson. Great efforts were made by the 'Society of Lovers of old Liverpool,' to trace the tea service so that it could be on exhibition during Civic Week. Mr. De Monte kindly consented to lend the cream jug, and it was put in the temporary possession of the editor of the 'Liverpool Daily Post.'

The tea-service was designed by Mr. Joseph Mayer, a Liverpool silver smith, in 1846, and the design was submitted to Queen

Victoria for her approval. It was also approved by Queen Charlotte, the widowed Queen of William IV, and the countess of Derby after which it was duly presented to 'Great Catherine of Liverpool'. The service consisted of a silver teapot, a cream jug and silver tongs, and a complete set of old china cups, saucers and plates each piece of silver was inscribed:

'Thou shalt love thy neighbour as thyself.'

Presented by the Queen, the Queen Dowager, and the Ladies of Liverpool to Catherine Wilkinson, MDCCCXLVI.

The great Catherine of Liverpool, is how the more privileged, in society felt about Kitty in 1846. Many Ladies of Liverpool had helped Kitty in her work over the years. Some of those women had been members of the District Provident Society, and must have come into contact with Kitty. The people whom she helped over the years had first hand knowledge of her work. Those who made use of the washhouses and peoples baths many years later had also been recipients of Kitty's efforts to improve their living conditions and improve the quality of their lives.

Kitty continued to be honoured. Six years later a thanksgiving service was held at Liverpool Cathedral on November 13th 1932. A centenary was jointly commemorated for two outstanding women.

One was for the inauguration of the first public washhouse by Kitty Wilkinson, in her own home. This was during the outbreak of Asiatic cholera in Liverpool. The other was the centenary of the birth of Agnes Jones who, chosen by Florence Nightingale, came to reform the Poor Law nursing system at the Liverpool workhouse.

The poor hospital was well conducted by Agnes Jones, who was appointed Lady Superintendent of Brownlow Hill Workhouse.

Nurses from London and other parts of the country attended the service which was held in the nature of a national thanksgiving service. The work of the two women was proved to have been of world-wide importance. William Rathbone, was also identified with the work of both women and was instrumental in bringing nurse Agnes Jones to Liverpool in spite of strong opposition.

Some of Kitty Wilkinson's methods of nursing were adopted by William Rathbone who approached the select Vestry (select committee) of Brownlow Hill workhouse and offered to put a trained nurse in the workhouse to replace the system of having the sick nursed by infirm female paupers.

He offered to pay all the expenses of the new system for three years. The offer was accepted and Agnes Jones, a friend of Florence Nightingale, came to Brownlow Hill as the first trained nurse in any public institution in Britain.

At that time, before Agnes Jones's appointment, nursing at Brownlow Hill was in the care of two women, neither had been trained as nurses, and their only assistants were pauper women. From the staff point of view this workhouse was no worse than most others in the country.

Soon after her appointment, Agnes Jones and the few nurses who came with her from St. Thomas's London attempted to train some of the able-bodied women paupers as nurses. Sixty-five of these were selected, paid a small wage and given the title of "Assistant nurse."

At that time infectious disease was one of the great dangers in the workhouse community, and on 6th February 1868 Agnes Jones fell ill and was found to be suffering from typhus fever. During her short illness, Florence Nightingale wrote to an aunt of Agnes saying:

*I look on her as one of the most valuable lives in England in
the present state of the poor law and workhouse nursing.*

Despite the care she received, the illness proved fatal, and Agnes
Jones died in the early morning of the 19th February, 1868.

She was mourned by all who had known her and, above all, by
patients in Brownlow Hill Workhouse for whom she had lived and
died. The remains of Agnes Jones were taken back to Ireland,
where the funeral took place at Fahan on the 25th February 1868,
and she was buried in the family tomb in Fahan churchyard close
to Lough Swilly, Donegal.

In the chapel of the workhouse on Brownlow Hill, stood a statue
of the Angel of Resurrection by Tenerari. On the plinth there are
inscriptions by Florence Nightingale, and the Bishop of Derry.
The statue was later removed to the chapel at Walton Hospital,
after Brownlow Hill Institution was demolished.

Gray Quill in his column in the Weekly Post, March 19, 1932
pays tribute to Kitty.

*It was not great Dickens who slew Mrs Gamp; it was
Liverpool, and the good old town did this through its
greatest woman who has left thousands of noble women all
over the world of the afflicted, in comforting the sick, and
consoling the dying.*

*That time itself can never erase from the proud pages of
man's history the story of Agnes Jones is noble her highest
praise is that she worthily continued the greatest traditions
of Catherine of Liverpool.*

The depth of feeling that `Gray Quill' had for Kitty shows itself
in a more romantic way in the same article.

*Woman outshines poets and warriors Catherine Wilkinson
mother of modern sanitary science.*

Kitty Wilkinson

A contrast in immortals this year commemorates many notable centenary anniversaries of wondrous births, deaths, and great events. Fifteen hundred years ago the figure of St. Patrick stalked across the world stage to perform one miracle which makes his many others far lesser things: he turned a whole nations worship from earthly fires to those lighted in a high heaven unseen up to then only by a prophet, and made men of lesser vision see with his eyes a belief that made them think that all their previous wisdom was folly, and their new faith a key to all the unseen mysteries which had haunted their hearts.

In one heroic gesture he tears down the figure of Baal from the altars of Ireland, and puts in their place the golden figure of the White Christ, to extinguish the fires of one faith, and light the fire of a higher in the eyes of doubtful men is a wonderful miracle. That it was a lasting fire was shown by the fact that the disciples of St. Patrick became apostles of his belief, and carried the fiery cross of his faith to other nations, but within the last century whilst the world rang with deeds of two great men, a great woman was quietly doing a world work almost unnoticed.

Walter Scott, the novelist, and Wolfgang von Guethe, left this life after strenuous careers which had a reflex in the world's thought and the world's action, but the woman unknown by name outside her adopted city of Liverpool has had more influence in shaping modern civilisation than all the world's poets and novelists put together. It may be that when her celebration takes place men will realise how great a good it was for the world that Catherine Wilkinson lived.

Gray Quill, once again allows his pen to flow freely in his article in the Weekly Post as he puts Kitty on a pedestal, alongside some of the most famous women that have ever lived.

In Honour of Kitty Wilkinson

Catherine of Liverpool, and her great work for Merseyside

and for the World.

Who is the most remarkable woman that has ever lived in these islands? The well-man turns over his memory, and a vision of great, wonderful, famous, remarkable, and even notorious women will flash across his mind:-

Boadicea; Queen Phillipa, who saved the heroic burgesses of Calais; the fair maid of Holland (Upholland, Lancashire), who was the mother of the Black Prince, who won the battle of Crecy; Queen Anne; Elizabeth Fry, the famous Quaker; Queen Victoria; the Baroness Burdett-Coutts; Grace Darling; and Florence Nightingale.

But the man who knows social problems will say that one woman, who made Liverpool the theatre of her fame, and made her work, far more important to her than her memory, imitated all over the earth, ranks as the greatest.

She is the woman who was the founder of modern sanitary science, district nursing, infant schools, workmen's social educational clubs, the pioneer of the anti-waste movement, and of a hundred and one activities that one wonders that she could compress them all in the narrow space of a life time.

The last of the wash-houses in Liverpool, closed its doors in October 1995, one hundred and sixty three years after Kitty Wilkinson had created the first public washhouse in 1832. The Liverpool Echo, reported the threatened closure of the remaining wash-house, in September 28, 1995.

"The last wash call at Laundrette."

Councillors are set to pull the plug on the Fred Robinson municipal laundry in Everton." You can see how progress,

175

had changed the name of the establishment from washhouse to laundrette.

Many people in the area still felt the need to use the facilities and a campaign by the people was waged for many years to save the Fred Robinson laundry. The city council felt it could no longer afford to keep it open. "More like a community centre where people meet," *said councillor Lady Doreen Jones.*

Taken from staircase window, Liverpool Cathedral.

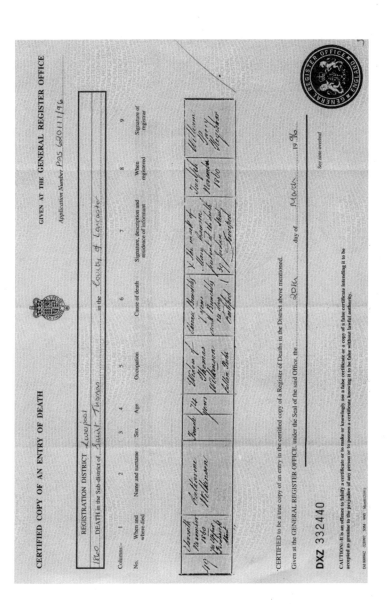

Kitty Wilkinson

CERTIFIED COPY OF AN ENTRY OF DEATH

GIVEN AT THE GENERAL REGISTER OFFICE

Application Number OAS 619142/96

REGISTRATION DISTRICT Liverpool

1867 DEATH in the Sub-district of Saint Thomas in the County of Lancaster

Columns:—	1	2	3	4	5	6	7	8	9
No.	When and where died	Name and surname	Sex	Age	Occupation	Cause of death	Signature, description and residence of informant	When registered	Signature of registrar
91	Thirty first October 1867 11 Nelson Street Frederick Street Liverpool	Thomas Wilkinson	Male	59 Years	Superintendent of the Corporation Baths	Albumenuria 22 days Certified	John Harwood in attendance 70 Upper Frederick Street Liverpool	Thirty first December 1867	William Harry Registrar

CERTIFIED to be a true copy of an entry in the certified copy of a Register of Deaths in the District above mentioned.

Given at the GENERAL REGISTER OFFICE, under the Seal of the said Office, the 5th day of March 19 96

DXZ 328682

See note overleaf

CAUTION:-It is an offence to falsify a certificate or to make or knowingly use a false certificate or a copy of a false certificate intending it to be accepted as genuine to the prejudice of any person or to possess a certificate knowing it to be false without lawful authority.

Dd 000542 328697 50M4 9/95 Mcr00 [2795]

Appendix One

The following are some of the orphans and families that Kitty and Thomas looked after.

Four Jones children taken in 1824, the father died of typhus; the mother six months after.

Ann, aged 11, went into service; later married Thomas Barker, dock gate keeper.

John, aged 8, got into Blue Coat School at 9; later joined the Royal Navy.

Ellen aged 4, went into service at Mr. Rathbone's when she reached 17; then married.

George aged 2, went into the Blue Coat School at 9 was later to become a tailor at Afflick Street, Upper Frederick Street.

John and William Wild 1827, orphaned twins aged 14, found sleeping in hayloft by Kitty's son John.

They were put into Seaton's paper manufactory for six months. Then sent to sea under Captain Finley of the Halifax. William was lost in a ship named the Grecian and John became a servant in America.

Three Dunne children, in 1830. The father worked at Fawcetts Foundry and lodged with Kitty.

Thomas aged 15, apprenticed to Mr. C. Hayes Block Maker later married and went to live at 68 Upper Frederick Street.

Betsy aged 13, went into service

William aged 10, got into the Blue Coat School after being with Kitty for six months; was later to become a clerk to a Mr. Cross.

Five Harrisons 1832, mother died of cholera, their father was out of work for a long time so was not in a position to pay for the keep of his children. Also Mr. Harrison made little effort to support his family. An aunt who had the children previously had 5s a week from the parish. However Kitty immediately stopped the payment on taking the children.

Mary aged 11, remained two years.

Catherine aged 9 apprenticed at 11 to Mr. Greg's Cotton Mill.

Sarah aged 7, Ann, 5, apprenticed to Mr. Greg's in 1838.

Elizabeth, 18 months died at 5 years.

The Coventry family 1832. The mother died of consumption and the father deserted the children and was never seen again.

Mary aged 8, was in Blue Coat School at 9 years.

Ralph, 7 Margaret, 5 William 3 were kept two years by Kitty and then sent to some relations.

Jan, 3 months died at 10 months.

The Hughes family 1835 on the death of the mother, Kitty and Thomas took in the father who was a dying man; he lived for ten months.

David was 3 years, Kitty got him into Blue Coat School at 9 and later started work at Fawcett's Foundry.

John, age unknown stayed with Kitty going to local school.

The Christian children 1835.

Thomas 21, dying of consumption lived three months.

William 12, bound to Mr. Dutchman for 18 months; went to sea.

Appendix Two

Betsy 10, got into Blue Coat School 18 months later she died.

In 1843, Kitty took in Tom Quin aged 10, he was allowed 2s from the Parish; this Kitty refused. Tom remained with Kitty for many years.

In 1837 an appeal for donations was put into operation by the Provident District Society.

A large proportion of our Labouring Classes live in single rooms, or in cellars, where there is no sufficient ventilation, generally sleeping several in a bed—-often with two or three beds in a room, sometimes in back cellars, where there is no air except what comes through the front cellar; few use sheets, and all wear the same linen night and day through the week. Nor will their small fire and crowded rooms allow them to wash their clothes without suffering greatly from the damp atmosphere created during the tedious process of drying. The consequences to health are found to be such as might be expected.

A cellar has for some years been hired, at No. 162, Upper Frederick Street, where from seventy to ninety families each week wash their clothes and bed-clothes, which are dried in a small room fitted up with a stove for that purpose, and are returned to them well aired.

These advantages are highly estimated by those who use them, and habits of cleanliness are greatly encouraged; but much difficulty arises from the number of applicants, as the cellar is small and low; considerably more might be accommodated by taking in the back cellar, and a different fitting up of both, at an outlay of about £20, and, of course, a weekly additional expense in coals and rent.

The necessity of cleanliness, and of a change of linen in infectious illness, both to the recovery of the patient and to prevent the complaint spreading, need not be dwelt upon; while the dread of infection, and the distress attendant upon illness, seldom leaves those most liable to infection the power of procuring a change. To meet this difficulty, for the last five years any infected clothes which have been sent to the washing cellar have been washed free of charge, and a change of sheets lent. A comparison of the number of sheets with the number washed, will show how seldom the sick have had but those lent them.

The weekly expenses of the portion of the establishment which enables families to wash their own clothes have been - rent 3s, coals 3s, soda 6d, with occasional repairs of the boiler, tubs, &c.

The additional expenses attending the washing of the infected clothes are - sheets to lend (which during the cholera required frequent renewal from many being buried), the superintendent, woman to wash the clothes, soap, soda, and mangling; these of course vary with the number of clothes washed.

The Washing Cellar has hitherto been supported chiefly by the Provident District Society, who now allow 10s, a week, and during the prevalence of cholera gave considerably more. There have been in addition a few subscriptions, but always inadequate to the expenses.

During the first quarter of this year, 767 sheets, 226 dozen of clothes, 121 blankets, 125 quilts, and 54 bed-ticks have been washed for the sick, and 709 sheets have been lent; in addition to which, 883 families have washed their own clothes.

The object of this paper is to ask for this support, and to prevent the painful necessity of refusing this small but important assistance to the various and complicated distress, attendant on infectious illness and poverty united."

Mrs. H. Jones, Rodney Street,
Mrs. W. Rathbone Green Bank Visitors.
June, 1837.

Appendix Three

Chapter 12, present at the time of her death, was a friend of Kitty, Mary Lawson. Mary could not write her own own name, the death certificate gave the mark of Mary Lawson of 39 Jordan Street. Could this have been the cause of the wrong age on the death certificate? It is also possible that the details given to the stone mason was wrong in giving her age at seventy-three.

Chapter 13, the memorandum attached to the back of Kitty's photograph informs us that Kitty was born on the 24th October 1785. She died less than three weeks after her seventy-fifth birthday, but according to her head stone she was seventy-three. However her age at time of death on the death certificate is seventy-four. This could well have been a mistake coming just a few weeks after her birthday.

Upper Fredrick Street, Liverpool Cathedral in background, 1999.

Kitty Wilkinson

Bibliography

Aston Chronicle May 19, June 2—23, 1849.

Boston Public Library, Department of Rare Books and Manuscripts, Boston Massachusetts United States of America.

Brown, Hugh Stowell. Twelve Lectures to The Men Of Liverpool. Liverpool 1858.

Daily Post & Mercury, Friday, April 1, 1927.

De Curzon Alfred. Dr James Currie and the French Prisoners of War in Liverpool 1800-1801.

Evening Express Kitty Wilkinson October 13, 1926.

Factory Acts, 1802 & 1833.

Finch John Junr, compiled and edited Statistics of Vauxhall Ward Liverpool, 1842.

Frow Edmond and Ruth, The Dark Satanic Mills Published by Working Class Library, Action Square, Salford, 1980.

Gores General Advertiser November 22, 1860.

Harris, W. T. Landmarks in Liverpool History 1940.

Holy Trinty, and St Peter's Parish Baptismal and Marriage Records.

Howson G.F Arcdeacon. Letter to the Liverpool Express Oct, 1926.

Hume A. LL.D., F.S.A Missions At Home of the Town Of Liverpool. Liverpool 1850.

Liverpool Daily Post March 11, 1902. Kitty of Liverpool A Humble Heroine.

Liverpool Echo, August 18, 1927. Kitty's Gift from the Queen.

Liverpool Echo, October 16, 1926. The Famous Kitty Wilkinson.

Liverpool History Of. Crane & Jones, Castle St, Liverpool 1797.

Liverpool Post and Mercury, May 8, and 20, 1932.

Liverpool Record Office, Baths Committee and Baths and Wash-House Committee Liverpool Record Office.

McNeill, W. The Noble Woman of the Staircase Window, and Atrium Windows in The Lady Chapel of the Liverpool Cathedral.

Newlands James, Borough Engineer. Report on the Liverpool Wash-house, 1856.

Provident District Society Report June, 1837.

Pumphrey H. George The Story of Liverpool's Public Services, London 1940.

Rathbone Papers, Cohen Library, Univ of Liverpool.

Rathbone R.Herbert, published edited version of manuscript by unknown author, A Memoir of Kitty Wilkinson 1927.

Rathbone R. Winefride, The Life of Kitty Wilkinson, A Lancashire Heroine 1910.

Roscoe William, Memorials of Liverpool.

The Liverpool Mercury, Cholera Hospital May 26, 1832.

The Liverpool Mercury, The cholera filtration of water May 26, 1832.